PRESENTING
Gary Paulsen

Twayne's United States Authors Series
Young Adult Authors

Patricia J. Campbell, General Editor

TUSAS 657

GARY PAULSEN

PRESENTING
Gary Paulsen

Gary M. Salvner

Twayne Publishers
An Imprint of Simon & Schuster Macmillan
New York

Prentice Hall International
London Mexico City New Delhi Singapore Sydney Toronto

Twayne's United States Authors Series No. 657

Presenting Gary Paulsen
Gary M. Salvner

Twayne Publishers
An Imprint of Simon & Schuster Macmillan
866 Third Avenue
New York, New York 10022

Library of Congress Cataloging-in-Publication Data

Salvner, Gary M.
    Presenting Gary Paulsen / Gary M. Salvner.
        p.   cm.—(Twayne's United States authors series ; TUSAS 657. Young adult authors.)
    ISBN 0-8057-4150-X
    1. Paulsen, Gary—Criticism and interpretation. 2. Young adult fiction, American—History and criticism. I. Title. II. Series: Twayne's United States authors series ; TUSAS 657. III. Series: Twayne's United States authors series. Young adult authors.
PS3566.A834Z85 1995

813'.54—dc20
                                                                95-32318
                                                                CIP

The paper used in this publication meets the minimum requirements of American National Standard for Information Sciences—Permanence of Paper for Printed Library Materials, ANSI Z39.48-1984. ⊚

10 9 8 7 6 5 4 3 2 1

Printed in the United States of America

For Kathy, Matthew, and Jeremy,
and for Gary Paulsen

Contents

Contents

Foreword

The advent of Twayne's Young Adult Authors Series in 1985 was a response to the growing stature and value of adolescent literature and the lack of serious critical evaluation of the new genre. The first volume of the series was heralded as marking the coming-of-age of young adult fiction.

The aim of the series is twofold. First, it enables young readers to research the work of their favorite authors and to see them as real people. Each volume is written in a lively, readable style and attempts to present in an attractive, accessible format a vivid portrait of the author as a person.

Second, the series provides teachers and librarians with insights and background material for promoting and teaching young adult novels. Each of the biocritical studies is a serious literary analysis of one author's work (or one subgenre within young adult literature), with attention to plot structure, theme, character, setting, and imagery. In addition, many of the series writers delve deeper into the creative writing process by tracking down early drafts or unpublished manuscripts by their subject authors, consulting with their editors or other mentors, and examining influences from literature, film, or social movements.

Many of the authors contributing to the series are among the leading scholars and critics of adolescent literature. Some are even novelists for young adults themselves. Most of the studies are based on extensive interviews with the subject author, and each includes an exhaustive study of his or her work. Although the general format is the same, the individual volumes are uniquely shaped by their subjects, and each brings a different perspective to the classroom.

The goal of the series is to produce a succinct but comprehensive study of the life and art of every leading writer for young adults to trace how that art has been accepted by readers and critics, and to evaluate its place in the developing field of adolescent literature. And—perhaps most important—the series is intended to inspire a reading and rereading of this quality fiction that speaks so directly to young people about their life experiences.

PATRICIA J. CAMPBELL, GENERAL EDITOR

Preface

"Jeez," I said to Gary Paulsen with a laugh during one of our interviews as he described his current projects and future plans, "slow down! You must be writing two at a time—a different book with each hand. How do you expect me to keep up?"

"Keeping up" has been one of the paramount challenges of writing this study, for Gary Paulsen, who at age 56 is well into his second hundred books, writes as if possessed. "I write 18 hours a day,"[1] he remarks, and the first instinct is to dismiss his claim as just another proud-author brag—a statement filled with the kind of hyperbole that all writers love and use. Hyperbole it may be, but then what besides long days of writing can explain that, within the past five years, Gary Paulsen has published 14 young adult novels, 3 major adult works, nearly 20 Culpepper Adventure books, several works in a new Gary Paulsen World of Adventure series for middle-grade readers, and 2 picture books? Eighteen hours a day begins to sound like too little time to produce the volume of writing that Gary Paulsen has published recently.

Is Gary Paulsen a driven man? Is he obsessed with writing? Of course he is, but I have been startled to find as I have met and come to know him over the past months how graciously this man wears his obsessions. Gary Paulsen might be a man possessed, but most possessed individuals are humorless, and Paulsen's infectious laugh seems always just ready to break over those around him. He may be driven, but most driven artists are secretive and withdrawn, and Gary Paulsen talks openly about the struggles and errors of his life. Finally, he may write to exorcise

his own personal demons—to "save his soul," but while Gary
Paulsen has had more demons to endure in his lifetime than
nearly any of us could contend with, and while he has certainly
used his work to drive some of those demons from his life, he also
seems to have had the immense good fortune to find, in writing, a
way of living that brings him hope and fulfillment. In other
words, while Gary Paulsen may be obsessed with writing, he is
also in love with it. While he may write to escape what his life has
been, he also seems to delight in and be entirely satisfied by the
life he has made for himself as a writer. Seeing the light in his
blue eyes and watching the sweep of his gestures, it is easy to
believe Paulsen when you hear him say, "I love writing. I
absolutely love it."

Many readers of this book will have come to know the writer
Gary Paulsen through his young adult adventure books, stories
of survival like *Hatchet* and *The River*, and books about dogsledding like *Dogsong* and *Woodsong*. Those stories have a basis in
his life, for the young Gary Paulsen spent vast amounts of time
exploring the woods of his native northern Minnesota, and the
man Gary Paulsen spent thousands of hours training and running with dog teams. The collected body of his work, however,
reveals a writer far more diverse—one with as much interest in
humankind as in the natural world and with as much respect for
acts of tenderness as praise for strength and bravado. Gary
Paulsen's novels reveal his interest in the arts, his concern for
social justice, and his passionate antiwar views. They also reveal
a writer wholly curious about what words might do and always
willing to experiment to produce various effects. While in the
rush of assembling words into stories Paulsen's experimentation
occasionally causes sentences to stumble or images to appear
stiff, even more often his risks prove to have been worth taking,
and his prose sings with cadence and repetition, his images haunt
with their precision. Gary Paulsen is a talented craftsman with
words.

Paulsen is also a gifted and tireless storyteller. This became
clear to me near the end of my first telephone conversation with
him in September 1993, when he derailed my methodical journey

through the events of his life by suddenly launching into a story about the "summer vacation" he had taken two months earlier—a road trip on his new Harley motorcycle with an old friend. Explaining that "I don't do things like sane people do," Paulsen told of riding all the way from his home in New Mexico to Fairbanks, Alaska, and back in 12 days, enduring mechanical breakdowns, 700-mile days on the bike, and hour after hour of menacing clouds and freezing rain. He acknowledged the awkwardness and comedy of having to say to his friend ("who thought we were going to camp and see the country") after only nine hours in Fairbanks and on the only sunny day of the trip, "Larry, we've got to go back," and he laughed about having to be "surgically removed" from the bike when he finally pulled into his driveway at the end of the ride.

During his recounting of this "vacation," Paulsen further revealed his natural storytelling gifts by giving a hilarious account of what in fact must been a highly dangerous incident involving a seagull. "We were smoking up by Calgary," he began.

> I bet we were doing 90, and there's this big seagull sitting on the side of the road, just sitting there. Big old seagull up by Calgary, and as I got closer he could see that there was something coming at him, and in classic seagull fashion he jumped up, and I took him right across the handlebar. He like to cleaned me off the bike—could have killed me instantly. It was like hitting a turkey, and I had feathers driven through my rain jacket. We measured him, and he had a four-foot wingspan. He was like a bomber.

After which Gary Paulsen concluded his account of the trip, after only the slightest pause, with the laughing comment, "It was a hell of a run. It was just great."

Which brings us back to the torrid and obsessive pace of Gary Paulsen's writing—in its own way "a hell of a run." For that pace Paulsen blames the Iditarod, the 1,200-mile trans-Alaska dogsled race he has run twice. "The Iditarod makes you not normal," he explains. "It becomes so weirdly possessive of you that it ruins your life." Of course, one has to wonder whether some level of craziness is not as much a cause as an effect of participating in what is called the last great race on earth. Does the Iditarod make one "not normal," or does it draw individuals who already lack a certain basic level of normalcy?

The drama of Gary Paulsen's life and the vigor of his personality have, in some ways, made this an easy book to write, for many of Paulsen's personal experiences and his various challenges as a writer make such interesting stories that they seem to tell themselves. But then there are those matters of pace and perspective—the feeling that another month taken in writing will put one another book behind, that another contemplative pause will take one out of the race. Yes, even writing about Gary Paulsen becomes obsessive, and maybe reading about him will, too.

Enjoy the trip—it's a hell of a run.

Acknowledgments

I am exceedingly grateful to Gary Paulsen, who generously offered his time and consistently shared his support and good humor during my work on this book. I also thank Paulsen's literary agent, Jennifer Flannery, for efficiently scheduling interviews and phone calls and for providing me with extensive background information about Paulsen's publications. I am appreciative of Youngstown State University for providing me a research grant and sabbatical leave to work on the manuscript, and of John Primm, who in friendship and curiosity about the project gave many hours to library research and the transcription of interview tapes. Finally, I thank my wife Kathy and my sons Matthew and Jeremy, who endured two years of my talk about, and preoccupation with, "the book."

Chronology

1939   Gary Paulsen is born 17 May in Saint Mary's Hospital, Minneapolis, Minnesota.

1943   Spends Christmas with relatives in Rainy Lake, Minnesota—the basis for *A Christmas Sonata*.

1944   Moves to Chicago, where mother works in a munitions plant. Is sent that summer to live with grandmother in northern Minnesota—the basis for *The Cookcamp*.

1945   Accompanies mother to the Philippines to reunite with father after World War II—recounted in the adult autobiographical work *Eastern Sun, Winter Moon*.

1949   Returns to United States with mother and father.

1950   Is sent to live for the summer with relatives on a Minnesota farm—the basis for *Harris and Me*.

1954   To impress peers, tracks down a deer and touches it—the basis for *Tracker*.

1955   Spends summer in North Dakota hoeing sugar beets, then working at a carnival—the basis for *Tiltawhirl John*.

1957   Graduates (barely) from high school in Thief River Falls, Minnesota.

1959   Enlists in Army after flunking out of college.

1962   Is discharged from the Army. Goes to work for aerospace firms in California.

1965   While working in aerospace in California, suddenly decides to become a writer. Quits job that day, leaves for Hollywood, and goes to work as an editor for a magazine publishing company.

1966   Moves back to northern Minnesota to write. Publishes first book, *Some Birds Don't Fly*.

1967   Moves to Taos, New Mexico. Begins to have problems with alcoholism.

1968   *Mr. Tucket*, his first young adult novel, is published.

1971   Marries Ruth Ellen Wright on 5 May.

1973   Overcomes alcoholism, but has to reteach himself how to write.

1976   *Winterkill.*

1977   *Tiltawhirl John.*

1978   *The Foxman. The Night the White Deer Died.*

1979   Heavily indebted, he moves with wife and son back to Minnesota to live cheaply. Is sued for libel.

1980   Begins using a dog team to run a trapline he has set up.

1981   Has a near-mystical experience running his dogs across a lake in northern Minnesota—retold in *Woodsong*, *Winterdance*, and *Dogteam*.

1983   Enters his first Iditarod trans-Alaska dogsled race. *Popcorn Days and Buttermilk Nights. Dancing Carl.*

1984   *Tracker.*

1985   Races in Iditarod a second time. *Dogsong.*

1986   *Sentries.*

1987   *Hatchet. The Crossing.*

1988   *The Island.*

1989   *The Voyage of the Frog. The Winter Room. The Madonna Stories.*

1990   Heart problems diagnosed; has to give up running dogs. *The Boy Who Owned the School. Canyons. Woodsong.*

1991   Moves to New Mexico. *The Cookcamp. The River. The Monument.*

1992   *The Haymeadow. Clabbered Dirt, Sweet Grass. A Christmas Sonata.* Begins Culpepper Adventure series.

1993   *Eastern Sun, Winter Moon. Nightjohn. Harris and Me. Sisters/Hermanas. Dogteam.*

1994   *Winterdance: The Fine Madness of Running the Iditarod. Mr. Tucket* (revision and re-release). *The Car. Father Water, Mother Woods.* Begins Gary Paulsen World of Adventure series.

1995   *The Tortilla Factory/La Tortilleria. The Tent. The Rifle. Call Me Francis Tucket.*

1. Beginnings: The Young Life of Gary Paulsen

As he leans back comfortably in a hotel lobby chair, Gary Paulsen talks about the experiences of his youth, and after a short while he comes around to describing the summer of his sixteenth year. "Home wasn't real fun for me," recalls Paulsen. "My folks were both drunks by this time, and every chance I got I would leave and just stay away." Paulsen tells of hitchhiking to North Dakota that summer, where he got a job hoeing sugar beets alongside illegal Mexican immigrants. "They would work me into the ground," he remembers. "They'd have a hoe in each hand and go down two rows at the same time. They'd be doing two acres a day, and I'd be lucky to do a half acre. Just incredible people, and then they wouldn't get paid. I mean, they were treated like dirt. Anyway, I got into a fight with the guy that owned the place. I left the farm and was hitchhiking and got picked up by these carnies, and I spent the rest of the summer with them."

This single vignette reveals a great deal about Gary Paulsen, both the person and the writer. First, it alludes to the extraordinary difficulties of his childhood, a time of living with abusive and self-destructive parents and of enduring great loneliness. Second, it acknowledges the roots of his social conscience—a lifelong respect and compassion for any "incredible people" who, like the migrant workers he labored alongside, are "treated like dirt." And finally, Paulsen's story of a North Dakota summer demonstrates how tightly life and art are wound together for this author. Readers of Paulsen's young adult novel *Tiltawhirl John*, after all, will probably have recognized immediately the basic

Gary Paulsen at about age four.

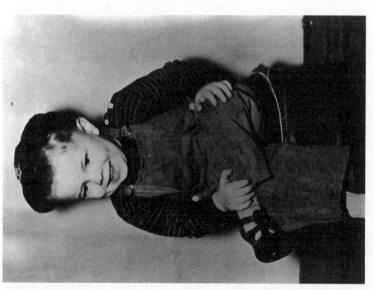

Gary Paulsen as a toddler.

Gary outside his parents' military compound house in Manila.

Riding a pony while on vacation in the Bagiou Mountains, the Philippines, 1947.

outline of his summer adventure tale, for this book tells the story of a boy who, at "fifteen and close as hair to sixteen"[1] runs off from his uncle's Minnesota farm, hitchhikes to North Dakota, works alongside Mexican migrants in the sugar beet fields, gets fired, and finally joins up with three carnival workers who befriend him and give him a job with the carnival for the rest of the summer.

"Mining my life is really what I do when I write," says Gary Paulsen. "I don't make stuff up much. Most of the things I write about are based on personal inspection at zero altitude, and I have scars pretty much all over my body to prove those things."[2] Because Paulsen uses personal experience as the primary resource for his stories, he has never been secretive about even the difficulties of his own life—reasoning that since readers of his books will likely discover a great deal about him anyway in that reading, he may as well be candid about his own life. As Paulsen explained in a speech several years ago, using his sixteenth summer again as an example:

> Writing about my childhood is the same as writing about anything else. When you are an artist, you spend yourself, and you hope that you've spent yourself just about out when you die—you've used yourself up. It doesn't matter if you're talking about yourself as an adult or a child or something you saw. There was a woman once—I was hoeing sugar beets, working with migrant farm workers, and a woman next to me, a couple of rows over, just laid down and had a kid, just right there in the dirt. And we all went running over there. I was maybe fifteen, and these old men—they were probably thirty years old, but I thought they were real old—they helped her have her baby. And after she had the kid they put it on her stomach, and she started scootching around on her back, digging her heels in, and trying to hide the baby, and I thought it was because we were standing there staring at her. And I said to this old man, this thirty-year-old man, "She doesn't want us to watch; she's scared of us." And he said, "No, she's trying to hide the baby from the beets. She doesn't want the beets to see the baby." Well, there is nothing in my life that is ever going to be as bad or as noble as what happened to that woman, and so to write

about my own problems is no more painful than to write about her. My own problems are really not relevant, except as useful things, artistic things. I don't care what you know about me.[3]

Since there is such a close connection between Gary Paulsen's life and writings, since personal experience and art intertwine in his works, it makes sense for any reader interested in his books to look first at the story of Paulsen's life, particularly the years of his childhood and adolescence. As one meets the young Gary Paulsen, one also makes ready to know some of his characters, themes, and plots.

Childhood

Gary Paulsen was born on 17 May 1939, at Saint Mary's Hospital in Minneapolis, Minnesota. His father, Oscar Paulsen, was a career Army officer, originally from Sylvan Grove, Kansas, who was stationed at Fort Snelling in Minneapolis when he met Gary's mother, Eunice Moen. Shortly after Gary's birth, his father was called to Europe, where he spent much of World War II as an officer assigned to General George Patton's military staff. Gary did not see his father again until he was seven.

For the first several years of his life, Gary lived with his mother in a Minneapolis apartment. He was susceptible to respiratory infections as an infant, and when he was three and four, he contracted pneumonia five times. One of his earliest memories is of being in an oxygen tent in his hospital room. The doctors, at one point expecting Gary to die, brought in a priest to give him last rites, and in a piece from the adult collection *The Madonna Stories*, Paulsen describes what happened next. "When my mother turned and saw the priest, she flew into a rage. . . . He meant death, meant to her that I was dying and she screamed, 'Not now, get out of here!'"[4] and drove the priest from the room. The powerful and terrifying look in his mother's eyes, the look Paulsen calls "the face of the tiger," was something young Gary would see again as he grew up with this fierce and strong woman.

In 1943, when Gary was four, he and his mother traveled by train to the northern border of Minnesota to spend the Christmas holiday with his aunt and uncle, who ran a general store on the shores of Rainy Lake. The story of that trip is told in Paulsen's *A Christmas Sonata*, a book that he calls "almost straight nonfiction." Gary's cousin Raleigh (called Matthew in the book) was seriously ill with a kidney ailment that would take his life a few months later, and so Raleigh's parents planned a special Christmas for their child. On Christmas Eve night, gathered around a huge tree that Paulsen describes in the book as being "so pretty it was hard to breathe, just looking at it,"[5] Gary and his cousin heard sleigh bells and went to the door. There, in the cold Minnesota darkness, they saw a sleigh pulled by reindeer, and seated on the sleigh, in a red suit, was Santa Claus. To test the authenticity of what he was seeing, Gary petted the reindeer and tugged at Santa's white beard. Somehow, in a way Paulsen still does not understand, his aunt and uncle had managed to arrange for a sleigh pulled by four reindeer and a white-bearded Santa to pass by the store that night, and for the children it was magical. "It's him," the ill Matthew whispers in *A Christmas Sonata*, and Paulsen concludes the story by noting that "it was him for each and every Christmas of each and every year that I have lived since then, and will still be him for each and every Christmas of each and every year that I have yet remaining" (*Christmas*, 76). In both story and real life, the appearance of Santa Claus that Christmas in northern Minnesota was a wide-eyed childhood miracle.

Shortly after that Christmas, in 1944, Gary and his mother moved to Chicago, where she took a job in a factory that made ammunition for the war. The next five years of Gary's life, from when he was four until several months before his tenth birthday, is vividly recounted by Paulsen himself in the moving adult "autobiographical odyssey," *Eastern Sun, Winter Moon*. It is a startling account, told by a survivor of a tumultuous and almost unbelievably horrific young life.

While his mother worked every day, young Gary would be watched by an old woman, named Clara in the book, who continually drank red wine out of jelly jar glasses and listened with Gary to programs such as *Fibber McGee and Molly* and comedians like Jack Benny and Red Skelton on the radio, swearing at the performers while she listened and drank. One Saturday, when his mother was home and taking a nap, the four-year-old Gary wandered into an alley behind their apartment and was accosted by a large, "dark-ugly" man, who grabbed the boy with the intention of molesting him. Gary's mother, having awakened, came out in search of her son, discovered what was happening, and savagely attacked the old man until he fell and then kicked him. As Paulsen relates in *Eastern Sun, Winter Moon*: "When at last his hands quit moving and he lay still she aimed careful kicks at his temples, aimed perfect, almost dainty kicks with the hard steel toe of her work shoes until he didn't move, didn't move at all."[6] Once again, Gary had witnessed the powerful and horrible "tiger" part of his mother's strong personality.

Shortly after that incident, Gary's mother began taking him with her after work to neighborhood taverns, where she would drink and dance with the workmen while Gary, standing on the bar, would sing songs and be given dinner and Cokes. One day Gary's mother announced to him that his "Uncle Casey" would be coming to live with them. Gary quickly realized that Casey (whom they had met at the tavern) was no uncle, and that he was staying with Gary's mother to relieve her loneliness.

In the summer of 1944, with Casey still in the apartment and living arrangements becoming increasingly awkward, Gary's mother packed clothes for her son, pinned a note on his coat, and sent him by train from Chicago to the northern border of Minnesota, where Gary's grandmother was working as a cook for a crew building a road into Canada. The story of that trip, and of the summer with his grandmother and a crew of rough but kindly workmen, is told in Paulsen's novel *The Cookcamp*, a book that he says is "almost exactly true" in its faithfulness to what really happened.

In *The Cookcamp* Paulsen tells of being watched by train porters on the trip north and then of waiting in the train station until his grandmother arrived. After riding even farther north through thick woods, grandmother and grandson settled into a warm, easy lifestyle at the cook camp. Gary's grandmother cared for him lovingly. She called him her "little thimble," sang him to sleep with Norwegian lullabies, and comforted him when he cried.

Young Gary spent his days at the camp watching and helping his grandmother cook for the men, feeding chipmunks and playing in the dirt outside the cook trailer, and best of all, riding with the workmen on the caterpillar tractors, trucks, and other huge pieces of equipment being used to chop and plow a road through the wilderness. From young Gary's vantage point, the men seemed enormous. "They kind of adopted me," he remembers now. "It was like having a bunch of bears adopt you. I was terrified and thrilled at the same time."[7]

During the months Gary spent with his grandmother, she wrote letters back to Chicago in order to, as Paulsen recalls it, "straighten my mother out." At the end of the summer, Gary once more boarded a train and returned to Chicago, where he and his mother would spend another year waiting for the end of the war and the return of Gary's father.

Paulsen's account of the end of World War II in *Eastern Sun, Winter Moon* reflects the anticipation that young Gary felt in 1945 that a new, more stable life would finally be beginning for him and his mother. "There came a day," he writes, "when all the people in the street came out of their apartment buildings screaming and laughing and crying and dancing. . . . Casey was gone and the war was over and Father was coming home and I didn't care about anything else" (*Eastern Sun*, 16–17).

Unfortunately, life was not transformed that easily for six-year-old Gary. Within weeks he and his mother received word that his father was being transferred to the Philippines to help set up a postwar government, and Gary and his mother were to join him there. After a hectic car trip from Chicago to San Francisco with two discharged soldiers, mother and son undertook a harrowing journey by merchant ship across the Pacific.

More than 100 of the 244 pages in *Eastern Sun, Winter Moon* tell the story of the trip taken by Gary and his mother to the

Philippines, and considering the journey's impact on the small boy, Paulsen's attention to it is not surprising. The trip was, in a word, horrific. Even before departure, Gary contracted chicken pox and had to be hidden on board until the ship sailed because he would not have received medical clearance to make the trip. Once under way, he was befriended by the rough-edged soldiers and sailors on board, but he soon learned that their primary motive was to get the attention of his beautiful mother, who by this time was drinking more and more and attending to her young son less and less. Almost halfway across, Gary witnessed a savage shark attack on military dependents whose plane had crash-landed in the ocean near the ship (an experience, Paulsen confesses, that still gives him nightmares). As the ship put in at Hawaii, Gary viewed from a distance the devastation of Pearl Harbor, and as he and his mother disembarked in Okinawa, they were surrounded by malnourished, silently begging women and children whose lives had been destroyed by the war.

In late fall 1945, Gary and his mother landed in Manila, a city nearly destroyed by the earlier invasion of the Japanese. Upon reaching the military compound where they would live for the next two-and-a-half years, Gary's mother was reunited with her husband and young Gary met his imposing, military father for the first time. The meeting was dramatically hopeful, as Paulsen describes it in *Eastern Sun, Winter Moon*: "He was huge, so tall he seemed to fill the doorway. He was wearing khakis with his hat off. His hair was black and gently wavy. He had brown eyes and he was smiling. . . . I held up my arms and he reached down and lifted me, lifted me like nothing, like air, and held me against his chest and hugged me" (130–32).

In the months to follow, Gary settled into the odd lifestyle of a lonely young stranger in a most strange land. Accompanied by the Paulsens' houseboy Rom, he played in downed Japanese fighter planes and tanks, rode water buffalo, and learned to eat baloots—duck eggs whose fetuses had been killed just before birth and then had been left in the hot sun to spoil before eating. On trips outside of town, Gary viewed a cave where Japanese soldiers had been buried alive and a prison where Allied soldiers were tortured.

At the same time, Gary began to realize that he and his stiff, military father would probably never become close. Both of his parents began to drink heavily, and he heard their drunken arguments and brawls night after night. The experience would remain part of Gary's life for the rest of his childhood and adolescence. As Paulsen recalled later in the reminiscence *Harris and Me*, "For nearly all of my remembered childhood there was an open bottle of Schlitz on the table. My parents drank Four Roses professionally from jelly jars—neat, without diluting ice, water, or mix."[8]

After a disastrous attempt at a family Christmas celebration in 1948, during which all of the family's attempts at togetherness seemed to dissove into drunkenness and arguing, it became clear that Paulsen's mother could no longer endure the isolation and erratic lifestyle they were living. As a result, early in 1949, Gary and his mother boarded a plane headed back to the United States. His father, after arranging a military transfer, followed shortly thereafter, and the family moved to Washington, D.C., where they lived for about nine months while his father completed his military service at the Pentagon.

After retiring from the Army, Oscar Paulsen took his family back to Minnesota, where he tried raising chickens on a small farm near the town of Laporte. Unfortunately, Gary's parents' drinking continued during this time, and so he would go to stay with relatives for short intervals. In 1950, when Gary was 11, he was sent to live for the summer with his mother's cousin and his family on a farm 40 miles north of Laporte. Gary's shirttail uncle and aunt had two children, a boy and a girl, and Gary and his 10-year-old second cousin spent the summer getting into all kinds of mischief. Paulsen relates the events of those months in the humorous, enormously entertaining, loosely autobiographical book *Harris and Me*, a kind of Tom Sawyer–Huck Finn chronicle of the adventures and misadventures of two young boys.

After two weeks on the farm, life settled into a routine: "Up, worry about Ernie [a rooster that would attack whenever they stepped into the farmyard], help with milking, and get in trouble" (*Harris*, 71). "Trouble" for the two boys included "going to war" by attacking the pigs in the pigpen, playing Tarzan by trying to swing on a rope from the granary roof into the barn hayloft, peeing on an electric fence wire, and motorizing an old bicycle and flying on it, out of control, down the farm driveway.

When their chicken farm failed, the Paulsens moved to the town of Thief River Falls, Minnesota, where Gary's father held a variety of jobs to supplement his military pension. He worked as a gas station attendant for a while and, unwisely, also tried being a bartender and managing a liquor store. With drinking still pervading Gary's home life, he again stayed with relatives every chance he had. Paulsen recalls, "In the summers I would go, and then every chance I got I would go. Home life wasn't real fun for me. I mean I shouldn't have been there, frankly, but there was no machinery for a kid not to be at home at that time. And so every chance I got I would leave and just stay away. And then I'd go to work with the relatives all summer or in the fall I would go deer hunting with them. Just every weekend, you know; I mean every opportunity I would get away from the house."

Significantly, these escapes from his unhappy home took the young Gary Paulsen to two locales that are portrayed warmly in his writings: the farm and the woods. Farms in Paulsen's books are places of hard work and limited resources, but they are also occupied by loving, close-knit families. The woods contain danger, but also beauty and adventure. Certainly, the wilderness survival exploits of Brian Robeson in Paulsen's popular books *Hatchet* and *The River* have their origins in young Gary Paulsen's efforts to survive in another way by escaping to the woods and waters of northern Minnesota. In fact, Paulsen made that connection in discussing his recent book about these youthful adventures in the wilderness, *Father Water, Mother Woods*.

From an early age, school failed to be a stabilizing influence in Gary Paulsen's life. In the Philippines, because there were few dependent children in need of schooling and because guerrillas still fighting against the militarily imposed government were attacking all the time, there was little regularity to school life.

Recalls Paulsen, "You might have school one day and then no school for six or seven days, and they'd come to your house to see how you were doing. You never knew what to expect."

This school instability continued when Gary returned to the United States. While his father moved from job to job, Gary moved from school to school. Recalls Paulsen,

> It seems like I fought a lot. I'd go to a new school, and I'd have to fight. You know how that works. So that wasn't particularly happy for me, and about the time I would get adjusted, Dad would get transferred again. . . . I was doing okay until maybe the sixth or seventh grade. We were back in Minnesota by that time, and I just started to fall apart. I just didn't study and wound up in trouble. I pretty much flunked the ninth grade. They went ahead and passed me, but I had flunked almost everything—particularly, I remember, English and algebra— and they made me take those over while I was in the tenth grade. It was just a courtesy, I think, but by that time I was one of those they were trying to move on through the system. And I don't blame them. I skipped a lot; I was never in school.

Gary's attitude toward school was made even more negative by his lack of social confidence. "I was a geek, a nerd, a dweeb," Paulsen recalls. "You know, the last kid chosen for sports, or never chosen actually. I didn't really have a social life in school." During his freshman year, Gary decided to do something to get the attention of his classmates. He tracked a doe through the woods near his home for two days and a night, following the wild animal until it was "blown"—unable to get up and run further, and then he touched the deer. "I thought," recalls Paulsen, "God, if I did this, if I did this spectacular thing, I would be popular. But it didn't work. Nobody believed me, and in any event, I was still a geek."

Gary's experience tracking a deer (a feat he says was "not really that hard to do" and was commonly done by Native Americans) later became the basis for the book *Tracker*, a story of 14-year-old John Borne, who tracks down a deer for a purpose even more urgent than popularity: to come to terms with the approaching death of his beloved grandfather.

During the same year that he tracked the deer, while Gary was still 14, he had another experience even more important to his future. One winter night in Thief River Falls, while walking home in 20-below-zero temperatures, Gary came upon the small town library. "I could see the reading room bathed in a beautiful golden light," he remembers. "I went in to get warm and to my absolute astonishment the librarian walked up to me and asked if I wanted a library card. She didn't care if I looked right, wore the right clothes, dated the right girls, was popular at sports—none of those prejudices existed in the public library. When she handed me the card, she handed me the world. I can't even describe how liberating it was."[9]

That night the librarian helped Gary check out his first book, promising that when he returned it he could have another, and so began Gary's experience as a reader. Over the next one-and-a-half years, this tall, thin, bespectacled librarian, whose name Paulsen no longer remembers, guided Gary's reading. "She started me with something like Zane Gray," he recalls. "I can't remember for sure, but it was a Western. Then she graduated me to Edgar Rice Burroughs, like *The Chessmen of Mars* and some other books he wrote outside the Tarzan series—science fiction stuff. And then, finally, I'd go in and she'd be giving me a couple of Westerns and she'd schlep in a Melville. She knew what she was doing. She really took the time to help me."

The reading made a tremendous difference to Gary. "I wound up reading to escape," he explains, "to get away from what was going on in my home. We lived in an apartment house and I'd hide in the basement by the furnace in an old easy chair with the springs sticking up, and I'd go down there with a quart of milk and toast and peanut butter. There was a light hanging from the ceiling in the corner, and I'd read and read and read."[10] In another interview, Paulsen summed up the significance of the experience with an analogy: "It was as though I had been dying of thirst and the librarian had handed me a five-gallon bucket of water. I drank and drank" ("SATA," 78).

Reading whenever he could, attending school as much as he was required to, and leaving home when necessary, Gary made his way through his middle teen years, graduating "with probably a D- average" from Thief River Falls High School in 1957. Certainly, he had already by that time survived a more turbulent childhood than almost any of us have known or would want to imagine. What was not clear yet is what kind of person that struggle had produced, and what the adolescent Gary Paulsen would do to further shape the adult he was becoming.

2. Lessons: Becoming a Writer

"Writing is everything," says Gary Paulsen. "It isn't just part of something. It is everything that I am" ("TV"). Certainly, looking at Paulsen's writing habits today and reviewing his remarkable output (more than 100 books published in 25 years), it is easy to understand what Paulsen means when he says that "writing is everything" to him. But how did Gary Paulsen come to discover writing as a career and a passion? How did the 18-year-old who insists that he did "absolutely no writing" in high school, and who graduated with a D- average, find writing and become such a successful, highly praised author? If the story of Gary Paulsen's first 18 years is one of survival, then the story of his next dozen is one of finding purpose and direction.

Fresh out of high school and wholly unsure of what he wanted to do next, Paulsen left Thief River Falls and enrolled in the fall of 1957 at nearby Bemidji State Teacher's College (now Bemidji State University), paying his way by laying traplines for the State of Minnesota. But college, confesses Paulsen, was not a good place for one as undisciplined as he. "I don't know why they accepted me. I honest to God don't. . . . I took pre-engineering courses, and the grades started slipping really bad towards the end of the first quarter. Then I tried another quarter, and that was the end of that—I flunked."

Gary Paulsen has gone back to Bemidji State University several times to lecture, and the first time back, during a signing tour for his first book, a helpful English professor he had while enrolled at the school came up to him in the signing line. While congratulating the young author, the man inadvertently summed up his original expectations for Gary Paulsen by exclaiming over and over, "I can't believe you got a book published! I can't believe you got a book published!"

Given his father's military career and Paulsen's recollection of playing soldier "constantly" as a child during World War II, it is not surprising that the young man's next career move would be to enlist in the Armed Forces. And so early in 1959, out of college and looking for a new start, 19-year-old Gary Paulsen joined the Army.

Paulsen sums up his military career this way: "I was in the Army three years, eight months, 21 days, and nine hours. It's right up there with hoeing sugar beets in my memory. . . . God, but I hated the Army." Still, for all the frustration that military life brought to Gary Paulsen, it also produced some benefits.

Paulsen's basic training was completed at Fort Carson, Colorado, where he had an immediate run-in with his drill sergeant. "You hear these stories," Paulsen recalls, "about the D.I., the Drill Instructor, and how he takes someone under his wing. Well, I was one of those guys. I mean when I went into the Army, it was not the place where you could 'be all you can be.'"

Paulsen's drill instructor, a Sergeant Gross, immediately challenged his surly attitude and punished him for his insubordination. Gross "decided he'd seen something in me worth working with," Paulsen remembers. "And he did work with me. That was when they could 'touch' you. They can't touch you anymore, but by God, they could touch me then, and he did 'touch me' a few times. I mean, I was a rebel. I was just stupid is what I was. And we finally sat down one day and he says, 'You know, you're wasting yourself.' And he really straightened me out."

At Sergeant Gross's urging, Paulsen "took a short" after three weeks—a kind of instantaneous discharge and re-enlistment that enabled the young recruit to sign up for an Army missile training program. For two-and-a-half years of his Army term, Paulsen took courses in electrical engineering and missile technology, the result being that he became certified as a field engineer.

Paulsen was stationed at Army bases in Colorado, Oklahoma, and Texas. Then in 1961, with 17 days left in Paulsen's military term, the United States clandestinely directed an invasion of Cuba at the Bay of Pigs. Although the invasion was quickly put down, the instability it created motivated President Kennedy to cancel many military discharges, including Paulsen's. He was sent to Fort Bliss, near the Texas border with Mexico, where for an additional nine months "we designed and shot these missiles that we were all going to go to Cuba and kill people with." (The same Fort Bliss figures in several of Paulsen's books. In *Canyons*, for example, the young Apache brave Coyote Runs was murdered by cavalry stationed at Fort Bliss, which was a military outpost on the Western frontier in the 1860s. Sergeant Locke, who befriends a homeless Mexican boy in *The Crossing*, is stationed at Fort Bliss, as is the young recruit in the story "The Soldier" in *The Madonna Stories*.)

Finally, Gary Paulsen was discharged from the Army in 1962, and using his engineering expertise, he took jobs in aerospace with Lockheed, IT&T, and Bendix over the next three years. Paulsen also married during this period, and his first two children, Lynn and Lance, were born. Then in 1965, while working at the Goldstone Deep Space Tracking Center in California, Gary had something approximating a "conversion" experience—an odd and, even to himself, startling occurrence that would for the first time, at age 26, turn him toward writing. Here is how Paulsen described that event in an interview with the author: "I was sitting in a satellite tracking station in California in front of a massive console and related computers. During an inactive period, I'd finished reading a magazine article on flight-testing a new airplane and thought, God, what a way to make a living—writing about something you like and getting paid for it!"[1]

Within hours Paulsen was hooked on the idea of writing as a career, and without so much as a night to sleep on the notion, he acted. "That night," he recalls, "I turned in my badge and quit the tracking station without notice. I had a company car, and I left that at a gas station . . . , [and] the next morning I left for Hollywood. I kind of fudged around on this résumé—implied that I had been an editor, really strongly implied that I had experience along those lines, and I submitted the résumé to different places.

I was hired by an organization that is still there that puts out about ten magazines a month—mostly men's magazines." While these sudden decisions seem as impulsive to Paulsen today as they clearly were then, his choice of Hollywood as a place to go was clearly thought out:

> I went to Hollywood to learn to write. Had I been in the East, I would have gone to New York, I think. I didn't go to be an editor or go to get into movies or any of that stuff. I really wanted to learn to write, and I needed writers to teach me. I didn't know anything. I mean I'd sit down and start to write, and I didn't understand why I couldn't make things work. It was like a chimpanzee with a socket set. I had some rudimentary knowledge, but it wasn't happening, and I could see that it wasn't working, but I didn't know what to do to fix it.

Gary Paulsen worked for the magazine publishing company for nearly a year. After composing and editing magazine pieces all day, he would go home and work on his own writing (mostly short stories) each night. Then he would bring those in for his editors to review the next day. Paulsen credits three editors, in particular, for helping him learn the craft of writing: Dick Ashby, whom Paulsen calls "a superb writer—the best I've ever known with using words"; Ray Locke, who also worked as a screenwriter; and Jared Rutter.

While in Hollywood, Gary Paulsen also developed other interests. He took up sculpting and once received a first prize in a local exhibition. He also worked occasionally as a film extra. "Once," he recalls, "I played a drunken Indian in a movie called *Flap* starring Anthony Quinn. I was on screen for about thirty-five seconds" ("SATA," 80).

Ultimately, though, Paulsen found it necessary to move again. "Hollywood," he explains, "is a corrupting place. It is extremely seductive. . . . People there have this incestuous thing they do where I tell you you are brilliant and then you say, no, no, no, you are much more brilliant, and I say, no, you are *really* brilliant, and you keep doing that to each other without thinking about who is really going to be looking at [your work]. . . . I got

caught up in that with incredibly beautiful people who looked
like they ought to be airbrushed, all actors and actresses, and
they'd be fixing your Xerox machine. I realized that it wasn't
healthy for me, so I left."

Without any money, Paulsen retreated to familiar surroundings—the woods of northern Minnesota. With winter setting in,
he and his second wife Pam (Paulsen had divorced and remarried
while in Hollywood) rented a cabin on a lake for $25 a month.
Paulsen wrote all winter, and he sold his first book in the spring
of 1967, a humorous adult nonfiction work about the missile
industry entitled *Some Birds Don't Fly*. Paulsen calls it "an
awful book." *Some Birds Don't Fly* was followed quickly by his
first work of juvenile fiction, *Mr. Tucket*, a historical Western
about a boy who is kidnapped from a wagon train in 1843 by
Native Americans. Gary Paulsen's writing career seemed to be
taking off.

With money from his writing finally coming in, Paulsen moved
back to California, bought a 22-foot sailboat, and lived on it for
about six months. Then, in late 1967, he moved to Taos, New
Mexico, which was already at that time becoming known as an
artist colony, where he intended to set up residence as a writer.
Unfortunately, the process would not be quite that simple, for in
Taos the alcoholism that had consumed his parents' lives finally
caught up with Gary Paulsen.

"I started drinking a little before that," recalls Paulsen. "In
Hollywood maybe twice at parties I drank. But in Taos, I really
went for it, and within a year or year-and-a-half I became an alcoholic drinker." Paulsen's serious drinking continued for six
years, from 1967 to 1973. By the time Paulsen was 33, he confesses, "I was gone completely—a bottom-level, hard-core drunk,
with D.T.'s and puking blood every morning—the whole works."

During these years Paulsen tried to keep writing, but his
attempts were fruitless, and so he supported himself by working
at other jobs—primarily construction work and heavy equipment
operation. He also remembers, with some horror, doing demolition work for a while during this time. "Demolition is really
interesting when you're drunk," he comments. "I'd be throwing

50-pound boxes of dynamite around. It's a miracle I didn't destroy the world—a complete fluke."

One very good thing did happen to Gary Paulsen during these difficult years: he met and married the true love of his life, Ruth Wright Paulsen. The story of that meeting, like so many stories from Paulsen's life, seems more the stuff of fiction than of ordinary life—filled with intrigue and surprise.

Several months after his arrival in Taos, after he had already started drinking and as his second marriage was coming to an end, Paulsen was standing in line in the Taos post office one morning when two men whom Paulsen knew to be FBI agents walked in. The FBI, it seems, had conducted a preliminary investigation on Paulsen because of some concern that he had divulged information about the U.S. military's missile program in his book *Some Birds Don't Fly*. Worried that the agents were again looking for him and that he might be in trouble, Paulsen felt the need to give the $20 he was carrying (payment for a short story he had just sold) to someone else for safekeeping, and he turned to the person behind him in line, a woman in dark glasses, and asked her to hold the money. After the agents left, he turned again to retrieve his money, the woman removed her glasses, and Paulsen looked into her "beautiful" eyes. "When I looked into those eyes, I fell in love," he recalls. "I knew this was the woman I'd marry."[2] The woman was a freelance artist and former art teacher from Colorado named Ruth Ellen Wright. Walking out of the post office together, the two struck up a conversation, and in the days that followed they began seeing one another. The relationship continued for more than a year, and in 1969 they left Taos together to return to Ruth's native Colorado. On 5 May 1971, they were married in Denver. They are happily married still.

Unfortunately, during his courtship and the early years of his marriage to Ruth, Paulsen kept drinking, and in a sense the drinking became more desperate. "I didn't abuse Ruth or go to jail," remembers Paulsen, "[but] I used to fight when I drank. I'd go to bars, pick the biggest guy, and just get the crap kicked out of me. I don't think I ever won a fight. I suppose it was a kind of a death wish."[3]

Richard Jackson, one of Paulsen's former editors, reflects on how important Ruth was to him during these difficult years. "I really think she pulled him away from the bottle," explains Jackson. "I take that back because you can't do that except yourself. But she was a tremendously positive and insistent force that he not kill himself" ("SFF," 8).

In Colorado, Gary Paulsen continued to work at odd jobs, and in late 1971 Ruth gave birth to their only child, Jim. Still, the drinking continued, and for an additional year the couple endured the strain it put on their lives. Then in 1973, on a trip back to Taos to visit and party with friends, Paulsen began to acknowledge the destructive force drinking was becoming in his life. In the home of friends Paulsen remembers passing out on a couch with his two-year-old son next to him. "I woke up," he recalls, "and he was still next to me. And I thought, 'What am I doing? I'm sleeping on a couch in somebody else's home, 370 miles from my house, drinking and laughing and thinking I'm happy.' And I wasn't happy. And I said, 'This is it. We're going home . . . .' All the way home I thought, 'I've got to quit this. I've got to quit this'" ("SFF," 11). Breaking his addiction to alcohol was not easy, however, and Paulsen suffered through several failed attempts. But on 5 May 1973 (Gary and Ruth Paulsen's second wedding anniversary), after seeking help from Alcoholics Anonymous, Paulsen did quit drinking, and he has not had a drink since.

Unfortunately, Gary Paulsen's alcoholism had taken a severe toll on his writing career, and now sober, he found he could no longer write. "I had fried everything," he remembers. "So it took me from 1973 to 1975 to write again. And it was rough. I mean, . . . I really only lived to write, . . . and when I found out I couldn't write, I was terrified, I really just was. But I studied and worked and studied and worked, and two years later I sold a book."

The book that broke the ice again was not one of his young adult novels, nor even a work of adult fiction. Instead it was a nonfiction how-to manual based upon his work in construction. Published in 1976, it has the distinction of being the Paulsen book with the longest title: *The Building a New, Buying an Old,*

Remodeling a Used, Comprehensive Home and Shelter How-To-Do-It Book.

For the next several years, still living in Colorado with Ruth and Jim, Paulsen re-established his career as a writer and, while not achieving huge success with any one book, managed to make a living at his craft. Although he wrote a few adult novels during these years—primarily suspense mysteries like *The Implosion Effect*, *The Death Specialists*, and *C.B. Jockey*, the focus of his writing remained on nonfiction. He wrote two more home repair books—*Successful Home Repair* and *Money-Saving Home Repair Guide*—and a study of the American farmer, entitled *Farm: A History and Celebration of the American Farmer*.

Paulsen also began writing again for young adults. He co-authored, with Dan Theis, a biography of Martin Luther King Jr. entitled *Martin Luther King: The Man Who Climbed the Mountain* and wrote a series of sometimes humorous, not always successful, photo-illustrated sports books for Raintree Publishers with titles like *Dribbling, Shooting, and Scoring Sometimes*, *Riding, Roping, and Bulldogging—If You Can*, and *Forehanding and Backhanding—If You're Lucky*. Paulsen also wrote the first of his books about nature and the outdoors at this time, a lively two-book series about wild animals he called *Real Animals*. In the books, subtitled *The Grass Eaters* and *The Small Ones*, Paulsen gives the first evidence of his respect for and sensitivity toward nature and of his abilities to capture the marvels of that natural world in language. Reviewing the works for *Booklist*, Betsy Hearne acknowledged Paulsen's "strong writing" and praised him for giving information about animals that is "presented neither clinically nor adoringly but respectfully and true to wild life."[4]

During the late 1970s, still living in Colorado and with his writing career re-established, Gary Paulsen made a business decision that he now calls "disastrous," a move that would contribute greatly to a second interruption of his writing career. He signed an extended contract with a new publisher and began to write books for that firm, borrowing heavily against the contract at the same time. What he discovered, however, was that while he was fulfilling his commitments to the publishing company, they were not fulfilling theirs to him. As Paulsen reports, "I wrote some books for this person who didn't mail the checks—he just apparently had forgotten how to mail them, and I went under financially. We lost everything. I must have had eight or nine judgments against me from all the lawsuits, and so we had nothing left. In fact, the car we had was a Pinto station wagon, and they were going to repossess it. I had $900 in cash that I'd saved somehow and had hidden in my pocket, and I put Ruth and Jim in the car and drove to Minnesota, just thinking if I could get to the woods I could live. I couldn't live anywhere else. We didn't have any money."

Arriving back in northern Minnesota in late 1979, Paulsen put $200 down on the purchase of a small plot of land about 14 miles west of the town of Bemidji, a place he describes as "12 acres of brush with an old metal lean-to on it." Of that retreat to the woods Paulsen recalls, "We got there in November and we wintered, and that was a rough winter. No plumbing, no electricity; a barrel stove with wood that we hand-carried in." Paulsen trapped small game for food, watched as the bill collectors actually tracked him down in the Minnesota wilderness and repossessed his car, and somehow managed to pull his family through the winter.

As all of these misfortunes were confronting Gary Paulsen, another career crisis struck: he was sued for libel. In 1976 Paulsen had published a young adult novel entitled *Winterkill*. The book tells the story of a young boy with alcoholic parents who spends time with the town drunk, is befriended by a mean, tough policeman, and is sent to live with several foster families, some of whom give him a life as difficult as that he had lived at home. Described by a reviewer in the 15 April 1977 issue of *Booklist* as "gritty and hard-hitting," the book contains less-than-favorable portraits of a number of adult characters, and shortly after it was published, Gary Paulsen was sued by a man he had known in Minnesota who claimed he recognized himself in the book. "It was all a misunderstanding," he says, perhaps too charitably, today, but misunderstanding or not, Paulsen received almost no support from his publisher during the ordeal, and the whole experience further soured him on writing. The suit was dismissed in a lower court and then again by the Minnesota Supreme Court, but it left Paulsen bitter and even more destitute. "The whole situation was so nasty and ugly," he remembers, "that I stopped writing. I wanted nothing more to do with publishers and burned my bridges, so to speak" ("AAYA," 169).

Paulsen's decision to quit writing altogether lasted three weeks. Having worked so hard to become a writer, he simply could not give it up. As he told reporter Kay Miller in 1988, "I had put the bloody skins on my back and danced around the fire for so long that it didn't matter if they paid me. It didn't matter if they sued me. It didn't matter if they shot me in the foot. I didn't have any choice in the matter [about whether to continue to write]" ("SFF," 11). Still, although he would keep writing, Gary Paulsen was determined not to be dependent on it and on publishers for his survival. At age 40, having already written dozens of books, he decided to change careers again. He would turn to other means of making a living.

As a child in northern Minnesota, Gary Paulsen had learned how to trap animals from relatives and friends, and he had turned again to trapping—this time as a source of food—upon his return to his native state in 1979. About the same time, he learned that the State of Minnesota had reinstituted bounties on beavers and coyotes as part of a predator control program, and so he set up a 20-mile trapline as a way of producing some income for his family, working the line on foot or occasionally on skis. The next year he continued the slow process of working the line on foot until one day a neighbor and friend, Bob McWilliams, offered Paulsen, for free, a broken sled and four dogs he could no longer keep. After repairing the sled and learning to run the dogs, Paulsen began using them to work his trapline, and with this new means of transportation he was able to expand the line to 60 miles. Still without a car, he also used the dog team to run errands, and before long he was spending hours and hours each day working with and caring for the dogs. Slowly he was being taken over by what he calls the "ancient and beautiful" experience of running with a dog team.

One night, coming home from a check of the trapline, Paulsen had an experience that overwhelmed him with the beauty and mystery of running dogs, an experience he would later describe in writing a number of times, including in his nonfiction books *Woodsong* and *Winterdance* and in the picture book *Dogteam*. It was close to midnight, and Paulsen was crossing three-mile-long Clear Water Lake with the dogs. "It was about 30 below," he recalls, "and the moon was full and really bright. I started up a hill through some Norway pines, like a cathedral. The steam from the dogs' breath came over their backs and hit them. It was like being pulled by a steam ghost. At the top of the hill I could fork left and go home, about 19 miles and two or three hours. If I hung a right, I could stay in the beauty. I ran for eight days. My wife thought I'd gone through the ice."[5] After that experience, Gary Paulsen spent more and more time running his dogs through the woods near his home, seeking to rediscover that beauty.

Paulsen's increasing love for dogs and for the natural world had another effect upon him: he found he could no longer trap animals. On a lengthy run he saw one of his dogs, Columbia, play an elaborate trick on another dog in the team, and he was immediately struck by the animal's spirit and intelligence. In *Woodsong* he reports his reaction: "If Columbia could do that, I thought, if a dog could do that, then a wolf could do that. If a wolf could do that, then a deer could do that. If a deer could do that, then a beaver, and a squirrel, and a bird, and, and, and . . . . And I quit trapping then. It was wrong for me to kill."[6]

For a while Paulsen continued to run his trapline even though he did not trap, just to give himself a reason to take out the dogs. In addition, he began to run sprint dogsled races in northern Minnesota for fun. Then, in late 1981, his friend Bob McWilliams told him about the Iditarod, the famous 1200-mile dogsled race across Alaska. Despite the thousands of hours he had already spent mushing dogs, Paulsen had no comprehension of what it would take to run such an extended race, and yet, intrigued by the challenge, he thought about entering and went into training for the 1983 race.

Ironically, the dogs and the race brought Paulsen back to writing for publication. The costs of buying a reliable race team, training it, and transporting dogs and supplies to Alaska would be substantial, approaching $14,000. It was mid-1982, and Paulsen had managed to raise the money to purchase a credible dog team. But he was in training, often running the team for 18 hours a day, and he had no way to earn additional funds. As the race approached, Richard Jackson, then the publisher of Bradbury Press, phoned Paulsen, wanting to know what he was writing. Paulsen explained that all his energies were currently devoted to running dogs and that he was currently not working on anything for publication. Jackson's response surprised him, and it also gave him the opportunity he needed to complete preparations for the 1983 Iditarod. "I'll send you the money," Paulsen remembers Jackson telling him, "and when you get around to writing something, let me be the first to see it" ("AAYA," 170). Paulsen's dreamed-for chance to run in the Iditarod had finally become a reality.

The Iditarod has had an immense effect on Paulsen's life and work. He describes his work ethic through analogies to running with dogs over sleepless days and nights, and he compares the writing of stories to the cooperative relationship one needs to develop with his dog team in such a race. Neither writer nor musher can be heavy-handed in his approach; both must be attentive to that which makes the run possible: the dog team, the story being written.

Although Gary Paulsen ran a second Iditarod in 1985, it is certainly that first race in 1983 that made the greatest impression on him. The run took him 17 days, 14 hours, and he finished 42d of a total of 72 original entrants. During the race, Paulsen ran without sleep, hallucinated, and overcame injuries to himself and his dogs as a result of the severe cold. He also kept a journal and took nearly 200 slides, both of which he has used since in numerous talks to young people and which he would later use in the writing of both *Woodsong* and *Winterdance*. Most significant to Paulsen of his accomplishments during the 1983 Iditarod is that

Before a dogsled race, Duluth, Minnesota, 1986. *Courtesy Duluth News-Tribune. Reprinted by permission of Duluth News-Tribune.*

he finished the race, that he was able to manage the entire run. Reflecting on the race some years later, Paulsen observed, "The Iditarod may sound like a macho thrill, but it's the opposite. You go where death goes, and death doesn't give a damn about macho. . . . Core toughness and compassion are the opposite of macho. The absence of fear comes with knowledge, not strength or bravura" ("AAYA," 170).

Paulsen's return to Minnesota in 1979 and his discovery of the wonders of running with dogs in the early 1980s brought him back to his roots, to the elemental nature of life in the north woods, and this essence is captured in the books Paulsen wrote for Richard Jackson during the time immediately before and after the 1983 Iditarod. First came *Dancing Carl*, the story of a man ruined by World War II, who tends the village ice rinks in fictional McKinley, Minnesota, and who expresses his emotions by gracefully "dancing" on the ice. Paulsen acknowledges that the main character is based on a real Carl whom he knew as a child, and that he had been working with the story line of the book for some time. In fact, *Dancing Carl* was first written as a set of narrative instructions for a ballet and was ultimately set to music by Sylvia Dierhaug, choreographed by Dr. Nancy Keller, and performed as a seven-minute segment on Minnesota Public Television by two dancers. When it was finally published as a novel by Bradbury Press in 1983, it was praised by most critics, among them Dorcas Hand in *Horn Book*, who called it "an insightful, beautifully written story, . . . filled with poetry and with life."[7]

Shortly after *Dancing Carl* came *Popcorn Days and Buttermilk Nights*, a romantically hopeful story about a young boy who goes to live with a "dreamer" uncle who is a blacksmith and who creates, out of old motors and farm equipment, a series of carnival rides so that the village children can have the experience of going to a circus. In 1984 came *Tracker*, based on Paulsen's experience tracking down and touching a wild deer as a young teen, which also received critical praise for, among other things, "a writing style that verges on the poetic, a romantic theme, [and] a sense of compassion."[8]

Then in 1984, while preparing to run his second Iditarod, Gary Paulsen wrote *Dogsong*, the first of his three Newbery Honor Books and perhaps the book that established him as a leading author of works for young people. To this day, *Dogsong* is one of Paulsen's favorites among the many books he has written. "I miss *Dogsong*," he has said. "I wish I could keep writing it. It's like a friend who has gone away" ("AAYA," 170). In fact, Paulsen has even admitted to calling the manuscript of the book up on his computer occasionally and rewriting sections, just to put himself back in touch with a book whose cadences he still loves.

Dogsong is the story of Russel Suskit, a 14-year-old Eskimo boy who has grown sad at the modernization and Westernization of his small village and who goes to live with the ancient village wise man Oogruk, to learn the "old ways" from him. Among other things Russel learns to hunt, work with dogs, and run a

dogsled, and then, after Oogruk's death, he takes off on a spiritual "dreamrun" that connects him with the elemental forces of
nature and helps him to create and sing a "dogsong" that celebrates his life and experience. Paulsen notes that the idea for
Dogsong came during his first Iditarod when, driving his sled
into a village for an overnight layover, a young boy came out to
stop his team and asked Paulsen to spend the night with him in
his family's house so that he could learn about dogs and sleds.
Explains Paulsen in *Woodsong*, "I [was] stunned that an Eskimo
boy on the Bering Sea would have to ask someone from
Minnesota about dogs" (129).

In camp training for his second Iditarod, Paulsen found the
narrative story line and the rhythms he needed to write *Dogsong*.
"It'd be twenty below," he remembers, "and there I'd sit by the
fire writing longhand in my notebook" ("AAYA," 170). The book
certainly re-established within Paulsen the writer's inner drive.
Despite previous lawsuits, financial setbacks, and long interrup-
tions in his writing career, Paulsen had again become the kind of
writer he wanted to be, one writing about what he knew and
cared about and managing to survive doing so. After *Dogsong*,
well into his mid-40s, Paulsen's income from writing finally grew
to a point where he felt he could keep writing without worrying
about the financial necessities of survival. In a sense, Gary
Paulsen the writer was reborn as he finally liberated himself
from those pressures.

Paulsen's writing output in the last 10 years has been amazing,
even for someone with his driving energy and self-discipline.
Since the publication of *Dogsong* in 1985, Gary Paulsen has written and published more than 30 books and many other articles
and short stories. After *Sentries* in 1986 came *The Crossing* and
Hatchet in 1987. *Hatchet* brought Paulsen his second Newbery
Honor Award and was made into a film entitled *A Cry in the
Wild*. Certainly it is Paulsen's most successful book, already having sold nearly two million copies. *Hatchet* was followed in 1988
by *The Island*, a *Walden*-like story in which 15-year-old Wil
Neuton (a character based upon Paulsen's son Jim) finds an

island on a lake near his home in rural Wisconsin, retreats to it, and learns to observe closely and reflect on the natural world around him.

Then in January 1988, Paulsen had an experience that challenged his 18-hour daily routines. Up until this time, he had still been taking his three dog teams out for runs of up to 14 straight hours, after which he would come home and write for an additional 4 hours. As he told *Minneapolis Star Tribune* reporter Kay Miller during an interview later that year, in January he started a run during a heavy snowfall, and about 20 miles from home one of his dogs cut his foot. Paulsen went to the dog, leaned down to bandage the foot, and almost immediately fell asleep from exhaustion. He slept in the snow for perhaps two hours, and when he awoke he realized that his legs were numb and his bare hands severely frostbitten. After sucking on a few fingers to thaw them, Paulsen somehow moved birch bark and sticks into a pile and managed to start a fire. At least partially warmed, Paulsen was able to line out the dogs and drive the team home.

The incident, while it demonstrates Paulsen's well-developed survival instincts, also reveals how Gary Paulsen the writer began to be gripped by a sense of urgency in the late 1980s. Approaching 50 years of age, finally having distinguished himself in a career that he had struggled at and actually abandoned several times over almost a quarter century, Gary Paulsen felt an increased drive to do the writing he felt he had in him. Instead of discouraging him and reminding him to slow down, the near-death experience with his dog team only motivated him to work harder at writing.

And work harder he did. In 1989 Paulsen published a collection of adult vignettes entitled *The Madonna Stories*, in which he sought to explore feminine perspectives on life. This was followed by two young adult works: a sea-adventure story entitled *The Voyage of the Frog* and the sweetly innocent novel *The Winter Room*, about two young boys who work and play hard on their family's farm, listen to the stories told by a great uncle throughout the winter months, and eventually come to discover first the disillusionment and then the almost magical fulfillment of larger-

Paulsen with friend and fellow young adult author
Theodore Taylor (author of *The Cay*).

than-life legends and stories. *The Winter Room* gained Paulsen his third Newbery Honor citation and continued the praise that reviewers had begun to bestow upon his works.

In 1990 three additional young adult books were published, and they reveal the range of Paulsen's experimentation with writing during this time. In the spring came *The Boy Who Owned the School*, Paulsen's first genuine comedy for young adults. That was followed in the fall by *Canyons*, in which Paulsen experimented with a dual viewpoint as he told corresponding stories of a contemporary teenage boy living in the Southwest and an Apache youth living in the same area more than a century before. Published at almost the same time as *Canyons* was Paulsen's first-person nonfiction work *Woodsong*, in which he tells of coming to know the natural world and relates the story of his first Iditarod race. By 1990 Gary Paulsen was also filling many days and hours with book-signing tours and, particularly, with appearances at schools, and in April of that year the pace of his lifestyle again caught up with him. Coming home from a tour of several schools in the East, Paulsen was in the Boston airport waiting for a flight to Minnesota when he experienced severe chest pains that he took to be a heart attack. Paulsen remembers actually being driven to his knees by pain, and several people stopped to ask whether they could be of help. Knowing, as he now quips, that "if I was going to die, I didn't want to die in Boston," he had someone help him onto a plane to Minneapolis, from which he took an additional shuttle flight north to an airport near home. He was rushed from there to the local hospital, where his physician diagnosed him as having had a severe angina attack. Tests revealed blockage of some small arteries leading to his heart. Paulsen was given a strict no-fat diet to follow and was told to cut back substantially on his demanding work schedule.

Another mandate from his doctor shattered Gary Paulsen even more: he would have to give up running dogs. At the time of his attack, Paulsen was in training for running a third Iditarod, and he was told absolutely that the race, and indeed, running dogs at all hereafter, would be out of the question. The news stunned this man who had, by his own estimate, put in 22,000 miles on dogsleds. At the end of his 1994 adult work *Winterdance*, Paulsen expresses the loss he felt then as he contemplated a life without dogs: "How could I live without the sweep of them? Without the blink on the horizon and the snap-joy of them and the reason they gave to life?"[9]

Gary Paulsen realized that his break from sledding would have to be total and swift, and so he promptly sold his entire kennel of dogs, all but his beloved lead dog Cookie. At the same time, to restore his health, Paulsen cut out most of his author appearances, and he reconciled himself to using writing alone to channel his still-tremendous energies.

In 1991 three more young adult novels were published: *The Cookcamp*, his autobiographical account of the summer with his grandmother and a road crew near the Canadian border; *The River*, the sequel to *Hatchet*, which has protagonist Brian Robeson returning to the woods; and *The Monument*, in which Paulsen combines his interest in art with his concerns about war as he tells the story of an artist who is commissioned by a small Kansas town to build a monument to its war dead.

The year 1991 also found Gary and Ruth Paulsen about to leave Paulsen's beloved northern Minnesota woods. As he explains with humorous understatement, "Without dogs northern Minnesota winters weren't quite as exciting." The Paulsens returned to New Mexico, where they had met, and found a house in the small town of LaLuz, about 70 miles north of the Mexico border. But still Paulsen was restless, and they returned several times to Minnesota over the next year. "Ruth was really sweet," Paulsen explains. "I mean, I was dragging her back and forth, and she was trying to figure out what the hell was wrong with me. And it was the dogs still. I missed the dogs and wanted to run. I kept thinking we could go back up there, and we went back in February [of 1992] finally, and that did it. We drove in the yard. It had been 65 or 70 down there [in New Mexico] and we got here and it was 48 below. We got a real taste of what I missed, and I finally realized that it wasn't going to work."

The Paulsens also tried living for a while during this transitional time in Story, Wyoming, but discovered (after the first, 34-inch, snowfall) that that would not work either, and so they returned to New Mexico for good in 1992. During all this time, of course, Gary Paulsen continued to channel his energies into writing. In 1992 he published *The Haymeadow* and began a series of books for Bantam Doubleday Dell entitled The Culpepper Adventures, very short, very funny books for middle-grade boys about two "best friends for life," Duncan Culpepper and Amos Binder, who find themselves in the middle of strange mysteries and exciting adventures. Later that year Paulsen published *A Christmas Sonata*, an autobiographical account of a Christmas in northern Minnesota, and he signed a lucrative long-term contract with Harcourt Brace Jovanovich publishers that called for him to write both young adult and adult books.

Paulsen's first book for Harcourt, *Clabbered Dirt, Sweet Grass*, came out soon after. Written for adults, the work is a sometimes nostalgic, consistently affecting tribute to the vanishing way of life of the family farmer, and it received immediate critical praise. *Publishers Weekly*, for example, described it as a "powerfully elegiac account of the seasonal activities of a multigenerational farming family."[10]

In the last few years Paulsen has continued to write for a variety of audiences. For adults he completed in 1993 the startling "autobiographical odyssey" *Eastern Sun, Winter Moon*, which recounts the first nine years of his life, and in 1994 he published an adult book about his Iditarod experiences entitled *Winterdance: The Fine Madness of Running the Iditarod* (a condensation of which also appeared in *Reader's Digest* in March 1994). For very young readers Paulsen continues to write Culpepper Adventure books at the rate of about one a month and has recently begun a second series of action/adventure books for young readers for Bantam Doubleday Dell, to be known simply as Gary Paulsen's World of Adventure. In addition in 1993 he wrote, and his wife Ruth illustrated, a picture book about running dogs entitled *Dogteam*.

Gary Paulsen also remains committed to writing for young adults. In 1993 came a comical, loosely autobiographical account of two cousins spending a summer creating mischief entitled

With the Blakely Bearcat kit car he partially assembled,
the basis for *The Car*.

Harris and Me, and in 1994 *The Car*, the story of a boy, abandoned by his parents, who takes a cross-country trip with two Vietnam veterans. Paulsen also has been seeking, as he has said, to "push the boundaries out a ways" from what is conventionally written for young people. For Paulsen this expansion of boundaries has included the release of works that are increasingly gritty and realistic. These include *Nightjohn*, about an escaped slave in the 1850s who returns to the South to try to secretly teach other slaves to read and write, which Paulsen wrote after extensive research in slave journals actually written during that time; and *Sisters/Hermanas*, a slim book printed in both English and Spanish, which tells the simultaneous stories of two young girls, one who is in the process of trying out for the high school cheerleading squad, the other of whom is a 14-year-old prostitute who works in a large Texas city after fleeing her native Mexico.

Gary Paulsen with "man's best friend."

In late 1994, Gary Paulsen left on an extended Pacific Ocean voyage on his restored 44-foot sailboat *The Felicity*, but even during this lengthy adventure he has continued writing. Due out in 1995 are a sure-to-be-controversial book entitled *The Tent*, about a father and son who take to revival preaching as a money-making venture; *The Rifle*, a book whose "main character" is a rifle crafted by a master gunsmith in pre–Revolutionary War days; *The Tortilla Factory/La Tortillera*, an English-Spanish picture book illustrated with oil paintings by his wife Ruth Wright Paulsen; and *Call Me Francis Tucket*, a sequel to his first young adult novel, *Mr. Tucket*.

If the first half of Paulsen's life led him, slowly but steadily, to the discovery of writing as a career, then the second half can be seen as the process of Paulsen finding himself as a writer. Today, after having been a writer, off and on, for almost 30 years, Paulsen almost without hesitation continues to surrender himself to the experience of trying to write. "I write," he said in 1989, "because it's all I can do. Every time I've tried to do something else I cannot, and have to come back to writing, though often I hate it—hate it and love it. It's much like being a slave, I suppose, and in slavery there is a kind of freedom that I find in writing: a perverse thing. I'm not 'motivated.' Nor am I particularly driven. I write because it's all there is" ("AAYA," 171).

If writing is "all there is" for Gary Paulsen, he has also found some peace and satisfaction in that single-minded pursuit in recent years. Perhaps that is because, as his work has been increasingly well received, he has no longer found himself necessarily preoccupied with the results of his efforts—whether a book will sell, whether it will put food on the table. Instead, and with great pleasure, Gary Paulsen has been able to enjoy writing rather than having written, to focus, in other words, on the mysteries and delights of the writing experience itself.

Paulsen returns to his Iditarod experience as an analogy for his love of the act of writing rather than of the state of being a writer. At the end of a video profile of him done by the Trumpet

Book Club, Paulsen says to the young boy accompanying him, "You're never going to be the same after this day, after tomorrow, after the next day. It changes all the time, and those changes are probably the most important thing in life. Achievements are nothing. The journey is everything, man. Once you're in Nome, what the hell is that? What's Nome? It's this funky little town on the north coast of Alaska. But getting there. . . . Wow! 1180 miles with a dog team. Whew, it's great! And life is like that."

For Gary Paulsen, so is writing like that—a journey in words based on personal experience and driven by a curiosity to find new literary Nomes. Admirers of his work can be thankful that, for Paulsen himself, the desire to undertake such journeys still burns inside. Gary Paulsen, having found writing, will certainly be adventuring in it for years to come.

3. Songs of the Earth: Paulsen's Survival Stories

It is said that every writer has only one story to tell—the story of his or her own life, and that each of that writer's works is only a different version of that story. With Gary Paulsen, the adage is close to literal truth, given how much his stories emerge from his own sensibilities and relate, sometimes quite directly, his own experiences.

In looking for patterns in Gary Paulsen's young adult books, one must recall those experiences that shaped so much of his life as an adolescent: the retreats to wilderness settings, both for renewal and (occasionally) for recognition; the search, given his parents' alcoholism, for other adults who would counsel and guide him; and the attempts to find himself, those coming-of-age struggles that often define a young person's efforts to reach adulthood.

Most of the young adult literature written by Gary Paulsen has one or more of these properties—nature settings, coming-of-age plots, and mentor characters, and any examination of his works is nicely organized by them. In the next three chapters these focal points will be used to review and analyze Gary Paulsen's books for young adults.

Paulsen's Survival Stories

In a review of the book *Woodsong*, the American Library Association's *Booklist* compared Gary Paulsen to another famous

Outside his current home in LaLuz, New Mexico.

American writer of survival stories. "Like Jack London," the reviewer observed, "Paulsen combines wild adventure and precise observation with intensely private discovery."[1] In its review of the same book, *Publishers Weekly* proclaims that "Paulsen is the best author of man-against-nature adventures writing today."[2]

Despite the variety in Gary Paulsen's collected work, and despite that perhaps only a fourth of his books for young people are pure-and-simple survival stories, it is these nature survival books for which Gary Paulsen is probably best known. One reason for that, no doubt, is the phenomenal success of *Hatchet*, Paulsen's best-selling book by far, and of its sequel, *The River*. Another is that quite a few of his books, while not purely person-against-nature stories, do contain some type of survival story line.

Certain features of Gary Paulsen's writing make his nature stories particularly effective and appealing to young readers today who have so little direct contact with the outdoors: the precise, almost photographic detail they contain about the natural world; the sense of authenticity that surrounds their events and circumstances; and the respect for nature that Paulsen shows in them. While many adventure writers establish conflicts in their books that are resolved by a protagonist learning to subdue or conquer the natural world, Paulsen's protagonists survive because they learn to respect it. Paulsen shows us a wilderness that is rugged and uncompromising, but also beautiful and nurturing. Like Paulsen himself, his characters make their way in that world by coming to understand it, respect it, even love it. That is why his survival stories might best be seen as "songs of the earth."

Six of Gary Paulsen's young adult works, in particular, focus on survival and the natural world: *Hatchet*, *The River*, *Father Water*, *Mother Woods*, *The Voyage of the Frog*, *The Haymeadow*, and *Woodsong*. Another six contain important survival story subplots. Taken together, they confirm Paulsen's reputation as "the best author of man-against-nature adventures writing today."

Hatchet

It has been a month since his parents' divorce, and 13-year-old Brian Robeson is preparing to leave his home in Hampton, New York, to visit his father for the first time since the separation. Since his father works in the oil fields in western Canada, Brian boards a single-engine Cessna airplane to fly across the Canadian wilderness, taking with him a small satchel of luggage and a hatchet, fastened to his belt, that has been given to him as a going-away present by his mother.

The pilot of the small plane says little to Brian, but after a while he shows Brian how the controls work and lets him fly the airplane for a bit. Suddenly, the pilot feels a pain in his chest, slumps over, and dies of a massive heart attack, leaving the plane on automatic pilot but also leaving Brian alone over the Canadian forests with no way to land.

Brian tries calling on the radio for help without success, continues to let the plane fly for several hours, and when it runs out of fuel points the plane downward and crash-lands it onto a small lake in the middle of the wilderness. Hours later, he awakens on the lake shore, badly cut and bruised, with the hatchet still attached to his belt as his only resource.

The remainder of *Hatchet* tells how Brian, a city kid with almost no knowledge of the outdoors, manages to survive in the woods for 54 days. During that time, Brian finds edible plants and berries, learns to fish and hunt with crude implements fashioned with his hatchet, survives confrontations with a moose and a bear, manages to build a fire by striking his hatchet against a rock wall containing flint, and survives a tornado that destroys his shelter. Brian is saved after the tornado partly lifts the sunken plane out of the water. In retrieving its survival pack, Brian unknowingly switches on an emergency transmitter, bringing a seaplane to his lake to rescue him.

A few subplots enter the narrative to enrich the character of Brian and to create suspense. One has to do with the boy's deliberations about his parents' divorce, which come to us through flashbacks and dreams. Brian, we learn, had seen his mother kiss another man and is anguished about whether he should share this secret with his father. Another is that Brian, totally unprepared as he is to contend with the wilderness, finds a way to extrapolate bits of information he has learned from school lessons and television programs, using these to solve problems in this unfamiliar setting. He remembers the advice of a forceful English teacher named Mr. Perpich, who would tell his classes, "You are your most valuable asset. Don't forget that. You are the best thing you have."[3] At first panicked by his situation and altogether uncertain of what to do, Brian eventually follows Mr. Perpich's advice and learns to depend on himself for his own survival.

Why has *Hatchet*, a book with limited characterization and a simple plot, managed in its first seven years in print to sell nearly two million copies? Even Gary Paulsen himself confesses to being perplexed about the success of the book. "I know it's a phenomenon," he exclaims. "It's incredible. I mean I've had letters from 48- or 50-year-old people who said they would've read books if they'd read it when they were young. I got one letter from a guy who was 43 who had not read a book since he was 13 until *Hatchet*. And I get 150 to 200 letters a day, and a lot of them are from boys who could not read another book until *Hatchet*. I honest to God don't know what I did."

Certainly, part of *Hatchet*'s success has to do with how Paulsen makes Brian Robeson a believable survivor, and part has to do with Paulsen's close attention to detail and his ability to make episodes in Brian's survival tale both credible and exciting.

The believability of Brian's survival results in large part from the gradual transformation he undergoes in the woods. Taking stock of his situation shortly after the crash, Brian is nearly overcome by panic. "Here I am and that is nowhere," he reasons, after which Paulsen notes that "with his mind opened and thoughts happening it all tried to come in with a rush, all of what had occurred and he could not take it" (*Hatchet*, 46). Slowly, however, Brian acclimates himself both to his surroundings and to his situation. After establishing a camp and learning to hunt for food, Brian realizes that he has begun to change, and that, among other things, he sees and hears differently. "When a sound came to him now," Paulsen writes, "he didn't just hear it but would know the sound" (105). Later still, after a tornado destroys his shelter, tools, and food supply, Brian mutters to himself, "I might be hit but I'm not done" (157), and in his new confidence, he even has time for humor. Remembering a moose that had attacked him earlier, he finds himself thinking, "I hope the tornado hit the moose" (158). In the book's epilogue, Paulsen sums up the changes in Brian and notes that certain capabilities he had developed in the wilderness would remain with him: "Brian had gained immensely in his ability to observe what was happening and react to it; that would last him all his life. He had become more thoughtful as well, and from that time on he would think slowly about something before speaking" (193).

Gary Paulsen has often commented that all of the experiences Brian has in the woods are experiences he has had: from setting up a primitive camp to being butted by a moose to being stabbed by porcupine quills. In fact, Paulsen's 1994 nonfiction work *Father Water, Mother Woods*, about his experiences as a youth hunting, fishing, and camping with cousins and friends, is the basis for much of what happens to Brian Robeson. So obsessed was Paulsen with authenticity as he was writing *Hatchet* that he took time out to see whether he could actually start a fire with only an axe, something he had not previously attempted. "It took me four hours," he remembers with pride. "And I ate raw turtle eggs. [They're] pretty rank" ("NA").

The authenticity that was so important to Paulsen in writing the book also partly explains its success. Quite simply, Gary Paulsen knows the wilderness and what it is like to contend with natural forces, and he reproduces those sensations through use of the most precise details. For example, Brian finally solves the problem of spearing a fish by discovering that the water "bends" light rays, meaning that he must aim slightly off center as he thrusts the spear. In learning to hunt the "foolbirds" (ruffed grouse), Brian finally is able to spot the well-disguised birds by discovering that he must focus not on movement, color, or arrangement of feathers, but on outline and shape. Brian sees the grouse as he learns to look for the outline of its pear shape in the brush. Small details, but they combine to provide a vivid, authentic picture of the wilderness.

Finally, it is Paulsen's respect for—even devotion to—the natural world that makes *Hatchet* such an engaging book. While many adventure books portray protagonists who survive because they are able to subdue or conquer the wilderness, Brian survives because he comes to respect, and even love, the wilds. After retrieving the survival pack from the downed airplane near the end of the novel, Brian realizes that it contains a rifle, and he is, surprisingly, troubled by having this new weapon. "[The rifle] somehow removed him from everything around him," writes Paulsen. "Without the rifle he had to fit in, to be part of it all, to understand it and use it—the woods, all of it. With the rifle, suddenly, he didn't have to know; he did not have to be afraid or understand. . . . The rifle changed him, the minute he picked it up, and he wasn't sure he liked the change very much" (186).

Hatchet, then, is a song of the earth rather than a tribute to man's ability to conquer. Respectful of the natural world, Paulsen has Brian, too, learn such respect, and this attitude makes the story, in this age of environmental awareness, a particularly modern tale of survival.

The River

> I wasn't going to do the sequel. But, I mean, we're talking 200 letters a day for five years or something like that, and that's a lot of mail. Thousands and thousands of young people wanted more about Brian. Brian had become alive to people, and I was holding back and wasn't going to do it, but then finally I got this call from the National Geographic Society, and they wanted me to tell them where Brian lives so they could interview him for the magazine. And I said, "You know, it's a novel."
>
> "Yeah, but he's a real kid," [they replied].
>
> They were absolutely convinced, and I said he wasn't real, and they said, "You changed his name, but he's a real kid." So then I decided that Brian had taken on a life of his own.

Within 43 days of its publication, *The River* sold 346,000 copies, proving Paulsen right that Brian had indeed taken on a life of his own. The public did want to know more about this wilderness survivor, and in *The River*, Gary Paulsen gives his readers more.

In writing the book, notes Paulsen, "I wanted to put [Brian] in a slightly older frame, so he could use some of what he had learned." And so, as the sequel opens, Brian Robeson is now 15, and it has been nearly two years since his 54-day ordeal in the wilderness. One day, three men appear at his door and, after verifying that he is the Brian Robeson who had survived alone in the wilds, make him a most unusual proposition. The three are affiliated with a government school used to train pilots, soldiers, and astronauts to survive in emergency situations, and they ask Brian, incredibly, to return to the wilderness with them, so that they might study his survival techniques. Brian at first considers the proposal to be outrageous, but after realizing how serious the trio's leader and the program's chief psychologist, Derek Holtzer, is about this survival program, he finds himself agreeing to go. Two weeks later, he and Derek board a small plane that will take them back to the Canadian wilderness, where Derek will observe and study Brian's adaptations to the wild.

"Just for emergencies," Derek has loaded the plane with all sorts of extra gear—rubber raft, rations, first-aid kit, even a rifle, and Brian quickly realizes that "it was all wrong," that to Derek "they were playing a game."[4] And so, as the plane puts down on a small wilderness lake, Brian convinces Derek to leave the extra survival gear behind, and to take with them only two hunting knives and a radio transmitter that could be used if a real emergency came up and they needed to be rescued.

Upon his return to the woods, Brian quickly recovers his survival senses and instincts. "He became, suddenly, what he'd been before at the lake," writes Paulsen. "Part of it, all of it; inside all of it so that every . . . single . . . little . . . *thing* became important" (*River*, 25). Equipped with these instincts and his previously learned knowledge about the wilderness, Brian is quickly able to establish a comfortable survival camp. He and Derek find a small cave to use as a shelter, manage to start a fire, gather berries, and trap fish. After only three days, to Brian's dismay, the expedition "had somehow turned into one big happy camping trip" (51).

Then one night, Brian awakens to smell rain coming. Almost immediately, they are hit by a terrible thunderstorm, and as Derek gets up to retrieve the radio and his notebook, he is struck by a bolt of lightning. Brian, too, is knocked out by the jolt, and when he comes to, he realizes the gravity of their situation: Derek is seriously injured—unconscious and barely breathing—their camp is destroyed, and the emergency radio has been ruined by the lightning. Once again, Brian faces a true survival situation, one that will require him to use all his heightened awareness and acquired knowledge of the wilderness.

Brian stays by Derek a day and a night, unsure of what to do; then he finds a map of the area in papers Derek has brought along. In studying the map, Brian discovers that there is a trading post about 100 miles south of their location, and that a river runs from their lake to the post. Realizing that Derek needs prompt medical attention and that the river current will take them south, Brian decides to build a raft that will float them down to the trading post.

The last half of *The River* tells of the suspenseful river journey undertaken by Brian and Derek. At first the pace is painfully slow as Brian learns to navigate the raft down the twisting river and through sluggish lakes. With Derek still in a deep coma and lashed to the raft, Brian survives groundings, hallucinations from sleep deprivation, and a race through dangerous rapids, during which he is thrown from the raft. Finding the raft intact downstream and Derek still alive upon it, Brian fights against the clock and his exhaustion as he again takes up paddling the raft downstream. After nearly three days and nights on the river, Brian reaches the trading post and the two travelers are saved.

Sequels, by their very nature, run the risk of being redundant and simply derivative, and in some ways *The River* derives directly from the pace and actions of *Hatchet*. Faced with life-threatening situations in both books, Brian learns to understand and respect the natural world that challenges him, and in doing so, he not only survives, but emerges from the experience changed. Some reviewers of *The River*, noting those similarities and other flaws, have criticized Paulsen's attempt at a sequel. A reviewer in *Horn Book*, for example, criticizes Paulsen for the "poorly conceived premise" that begins the book and for lacking, in the book's episodes, the authenticity that made *Hatchet* so successful as an adventure story.[5] Others, however, have praised the sequel, and have complimented Paulsen for taking Brian into new territory in *The River*. *Publishers Weekly*, for example, concluded that "the new adventure is as riveting as its predecessor and yet, because of significant differences in the nature of its dramatic tension, is not merely a clone."[6]

Perhaps there is something worth noting in both reviews. To be sure, getting Brian back into the woods in the service of a nonexistent government survival agency is a contrivance, and it does soften the beginning of the adventure. Yet once Brian re-enters the wilderness, which happens after only about 20 pages, the specificity of detail that distinguished *Hatchet* reappears. Brian finds new uses for the knife that he has on this adventure, and he notes the location of grubworms they may soon need to eat. ["You don't chew them," Brian instructs Derek. "But if you wrap them in leaves and swallow them whole . . ." (*River*, 41).] And when Brian launches his crudely built raft onto Necktie River, the pace quickens and Paulsen delivers a fair measure of suspense.

That Brian Robeson in *The River* is now an experienced survival expert gives the story additional texture in several ways. One comes in the role reversal that occurs between Brian and Derek. Once they hit the wilderness, it is Brian who is the teacher and Derek who becomes the student. Despite his own survival experience, Derek takes his lead from Brian, and this sobers the young survivor and makes him, if anything, even more introspective. Another result of Brian's prior experience is that he has now attained the maturity to become accountable for another human being. In *Hatchet* Brian has no one to worry about but himself, except for the recurring thoughts he has about his parents' divorce. At the end of that book he decides not to intrude into their decisions, showing that he understands his possible impact on others' lives, an important discovery for any adolescent to make. This realization, in a sense, prepares him to accept responsibility for Derek's life in the sequel after the psychologist is struck by lightning.

Finally, *The River* does succeed in reinforcing an important Paulsen theme: the sanctity of the wild and the need to enter it on its own terms. Once again in *The River*, Brian finds himself learning how to accommodate to the wilderness, rather than to subdue it. He realizes again that, to survive, he must "become part of the woods, an animal" (19), rather than become a master over it. In this way, and through the vivid descriptions of lakes, forests, and animals that Paulsen provides, *The River* becomes, too, a song of the earth that celebrates the natural world and makes man, at best, but a humble visitor in it.

Father Water, Mother Woods

Gary Paulsen explains his motive for writing *Father Water, Mother Woods* in the book's foreword. "In the thirty to forty thousand letters a year that come asking about *Hatchet*," he writes, "there are many diversities. . . . But there is one thread that permeates nearly all the letters. Almost without exception there is an overwhelming desire to know how it all started, where *Hatchet* began."[7] This autobiographical collection of "Essays on Fishing and Hunting in the North Woods" (the book's subtitle) sets out in search of that beginning, and in doing so it does manage to reveal the inspiration for Brian Robeson's gritty inventiveness and his respect for the natural world.

Later in the foreword Paulsen states that the poverty and desperate home lives he and his childhood friends experienced drove them "in a kind of self-fostering" (*Father*, x) to the woods and lakes of northern Minnesota. "In the normal run of things," he explains, "our lives hurt. When we were in the woods or fishing on the rivers and lakes our lives didn't hurt" (xi). "Adopted" by these natural environs, the boys found within themselves the curiosity and mischief of childhood. And Gary Paulsen found that place of solitude and joy that would later become Brian Robeson's place: the natural world.

Father Water, Mother Woods's 17 essays are filled with boyhood adventure and ingenuity. The first dozen pieces recount the boys' fishing escapades throughout the seasons—from illegally snagging northern pike and carp in the early spring off the dam outside of town, to fly fishing with homemade flies, to lazy summer bobber fishing [where "the fish are a minor part of it, a thing to justify lying back on a summer bank in deep grass watching clouds make summer pictures in the sky" (89)], to ice fishing in the deep cold of winter on the rivers and lakes of northern Minnesota.

The "Fishing" section is followed by one on "Camping"—actually a single extended essay that recounts a camping trip Paulsen and his friends undertook one summer. The episode is one of the most enjoyable in the book—filled with the boyish comedy that Brian Robeson also occasionally reveals in *Hatchet* and *The*

River. The fun begins when the boys learn, as they load an old bait boat that they expect to float downriver to the wilds outside of town, that they must bring along Gilson, an exchange student from South America who is visiting in the town (and who seems to know only a few swear words in English). The misadventures continue as the boat, miles from home, suddenly hits a snag and sinks, forcing the boys to hike back upriver through dense scrub growth, all the while trying to comfort their foreign compatriot, who is terrified that they will be devoured by snakes. Forced to sleep out under the stars before reaching home, the weary boys sit around a campfire and rediscover the humor of their situation—of how Gilson, for example, blazed such an effective trail through the dense undergrowth when he spotted a garter snake, and of how lucky they were that he happened to be going in the right direction. One of the boys mutters as they get ready for sleep, "Hell, this is fun. Where [are] we going to sink next year?" (*Father*, 126).

Father Water, Mother Woods concludes with four "Hunting" essays, and it is here that the roots of *Hatchet* and *The River* are most visible. Paulsen and his friends hunt deer, mallard ducks, and ruffed grouse (the "foolbirds" Brian encounters in *Hatchet*), and they soon come to prefer bows and arrows to the .22 single-shot rifles that "remove the animal from consideration in a way [and] make the activity less hunting and more killing" (*Father*, 164). The boys' preferences sound much like Brian's. Upon discovering a rifle in the plane's survival pack near the end of *Hatchet*, Brian puts it away because it "somehow removed him from everything around him" (*Hatchet*, 186).

The "Hunting" section also resembles *Hatchet* and *The River* in that it captures the same sense of awe and respect for nature that develops in Brian during his exploits. Near the end of the book, for example, as Paulsen describes the difficulty of tracking a deer and shooting even a single arrow at it, he pauses to reflect on the significance of that challenge, revealing at the same time some of his acquired love for the outdoors. "Sometimes a whole season can be spent looking, waiting, hunting for nothing," he explains;

nothing except walking through the beauty of autumn days in the thick forest, moving through color and clean air and the soft light of a million dappled leaves while the act of hunting forces all the things seen, all the beauty, into the mind. . . . [B]ut it is not until later, until years and a life later, that it is understood . . . that the reason for hunting is not the deer, has never been the deer, never would be the deer; the reason for hunting is just that: to hunt. To hunt the sun, the wind, the trees—to hunt the beauty. (*Father*, 176)

Father Water, Mother Woods is unevenly written, slowed unnecessarily at times by Paulsen's overuse of the passive voice as a means of converting these autobiographical anecdotes into essays—as in the passage "If the daredevil [lure] was used it had to be allowed to wobble down into the water . . . " (33). Still, in its liveliest sections *Father Water, Mother Woods* clearly delivers on Gary Paulsen's promise to connect his readers with Brian Robeson's beginnings. In the inventiveness of the young Paulsen and his chums as they fashion homemade lures and make their own bows and arrows, Brian's resourcefulness is captured. And in Paulsen's evocation of the comfort and solitude of the wilds, Brian's acquired respect and love for the woods is immediately recognizable. In those evocations the book fulfills its promise as another of Gary Paulsen's songs of the earth.

The Voyage of the Frog

Gary Paulsen's knowledge of the outdoors is not limited to the wilderness areas described in books like *Hatchet*, *The River*, and *Father Water, Mother Woods*. At two different times in his life, for example, he has owned large sailing yachts and sailed them on the Pacific. In 1967, after selling his first two books, Paulsen returned from northern Minnesota to California, bought a 22-foot sailboat, and lived on it for about six months. And then in the mid-1970s, after signing an extended contract with a new publisher, Paulsen again purchased a boat, a 26-footer, and drove with his wife Ruth and son Jim from Colorado to California to take the boat for a sail.

Ruth had had little experience on boats at the time of that journey. (Paulsen recalls her looking at a map and asking, "So you want to go on the blue part?") And so, to reassure his wife of the trip's safety, Gary Paulsen took all the precautions possible before setting sail—checking travel conditions with the weather service, for example, and filing a trip plan with the Coast Guard. Those preparations completed, he sailed the boat out of the harbor with Ruth and Jim aboard for an easy run from Ventura down to San Diego, where they planned to meet Ruth's mother for Christmas.

After sailing the boat 30 or 40 miles out into the ocean, Paulsen was just preparing to turn the boat south for the run to San Diego when the only hurricane-class storm to hit that part of the Pacific in many years struck. To save the boat, Paulsen turned it out to sea and rode out the storm for 18 hours, suffering severe seasickness all the while (and also, he quips, nearly bringing his marriage to a swift breakup).

The storm Paulsen and his family rode through is recounted vividly in the story *The Voyage of the Frog*. In the book 14-year-old David Alspeth inherits the 22-foot sailboat *Frog* from his Uncle Owen, who has just died of cancer. The two had sailed together often on the boat, and Owen wanted his nephew to have it, asking only that David sail the boat out to sea just after his death to scatter Owen's ashes upon the Pacific Ocean he loved so much.

While David has never taken the boat out alone before, he is an experienced sailor, and so about midnight, he guides the boat out of the Ventura harbor, bent upon honoring his uncle's last wish. By nine in the morning, far out at sea, David releases Owen's ashes, and then just as he is ready to come about for the return to the harbor, the *Frog* is hit by a terrific storm. For nearly an entire day, David fights to keep the boat afloat. He barely manages to get the sails down, is struck on the head by the boom as the wind suddenly flips it, and when he regains consciousness, is barely able to work the boat's pump quickly enough to keep the boat from sinking.

Twenty-four hours later the wind finally subsides, and David finds that he has been driven far off course and is perhaps 300 miles out into the ocean, alone in a disabled boat. For several days he sets to repairing the boat's damage, all the while coming to terms with his grave situation. After the storm, a total absence of wind leaves him becalmed, and he has to begin rationing the small amount of food and water he has on board. One morning, the boat is attacked by sharks, who actually ram themselves into its hull. The next night, after inadvertently drifting into the middle of a shipping channel, the *Frog* is almost swamped by a passing ocean freighter, which does not even see the small boat in the deep darkness.

After drifting for days, the wind returns and David again takes control of his ship, and his fate. Steering the *Frog* east, he encounters a pod of four killer whales, who playfully accompany the boat for hours, and he once again experiences the joy of sailing, of "turn[ing] the force of the wind and sea, the force of the earth and a person, into a dance across the water."[8]

As the *Frog* finally reaches land, David realizes how far south he has been blown and discovers himself now off the coast of Mexico's Baja Peninsula. He puts in at a deserted bay, where overnight he is again joined by whales. Setting off the next morning, on his way north to California, David and the *Frog* again encounter a storm, but this time David is able to ride it out expertly. Shortly after, he meets a research ship and is finally rescued. After being told, however, that he will have to abandon the *Frog* because it cannot be towed by the other ship, David decides instead to sail his craft back home himself. Outfitted with additional supplies, nine days after first leaving Ventura, David once again sets sail alone in the *Frog*, this time confident of his abilities and ready for anything he might face. "The *Frog* hummed to him through the tiller," writes Paulsen at the end of the book, "a song from the water that told him he could stow the food later. Now there was the wind and the sea and the *Frog*. He had some sailing to do" (*Voyage*, 141).

The Voyage of the Frog follows the same sort of story line used in Gary Paulsen's wilderness survival stories. In each a young boy, largely unknowledgeable about the natural world, finds himself in an environment that threatens his very life. Through coming to respect and learn from that world, the boy is able to survive in it and to become stronger and more mature as a result of the experience.

One part of this scenario that is worked out with particular care in *The Voyage of the Frog* is the boy's "schooling" in the world that surrounds him. Once David accepts that he is stranded far out into the ocean on a small boat and works through his anger that such a thing should happen to him, he begins to take positive steps to ensure his survival. For example, he sets up a routine for completing necessary daily tasks (cleaning the ship, eating, exercising) and, while doing so, realizes that something besides the normal chores also needs to be made a part of each day: "A learning time. Another thought from the night before, one that must have come while he was sleeping. He had to know more or he wouldn't make it. He should try to learn each day" (98). Uncertain as to how he will learn without books or teachers, David looks out at the sea as his mind wanders. "Could I study myself?" he wonders. "Can it be done?" (99). And David determines to study self and surroundings every day, as part of his coming to terms with the natural world around him and, in particular, with his place in that world.

In the same way that David sets himself up for a series of learning opportunities, Gary Paulsen sets up his readers to be instructed about sea survival. This educational function of *The Voyage of the Frog* is evident from the very beginning of the book where, before the story even begins, Paulsen presents us with a drawing of the *Frog* on which is labeled the essential parts and locations on a sailing ship (for example, bow, forward hatch, stanchion, jib sail, forestay, and tiller). Paulsen also allows his readers to learn about the sea as David learns. At one point, for instance, David finds an odd-looking cone net on board that he cannot guess the use of. A day later, however, he comes across a ship's log that Uncle Owen had kept since purchasing the *Frog* and learns, in reading the log, that the cone is actually a net that can be used to capture tiny, edible plankton, or krill, from the sea. Paulsen also passes along information about the sea by having David summon up past knowledge, just as Brian in *Hatchet* recalled useful bits of information heard in school or on television. While being accompanied by killer whales, for example, Paulsen says of David that "somewhere he'd heard that they could swim twenty to thirty knots an hour" (*Voyage*, 109).

The theme that we survive in the natural world by becoming one with it also surfaces in *The Voyage of the Frog*. After the storm, as David begins sailing again, he is captivated by the joy of his movement over the water. At first he senses himself becoming one with the *Frog*—"he could no longer draw a line where he ended and the *Frog* began," and then shortly thereafter he also feels himself combining with the forces of nature. "They were together," Paulsen writes, "a thing of the sea and the wind and man all joined in a single dance" (*Voyage*, 113).

Critics have praised *The Voyage of the Frog* both for being action-filled and for what Connie Tyrrell Burns in *School Library Journal* called its "spare, dramatic style."[9] A reviewer in the *Bulletin of the Center for Children's Books* likens Paulsen's style to that of Hemingway—noting, in particular, Paulsen's use of short sentences, dramatic pauses, and repeated phrases.[10] To be sure, Paulsen again in this book excels at re-creating the tensions of survival. Chapter endings, for instance, often leave the reader at the edge of a dramatic event, wondering what will happen next. At the end of chapter 10, for example, Paulsen introduces the next crisis in David's survival with the abrupt final sentence, "The oil tanker came about midnight" (*Voyage*, 84). Certainly, *The Voyage of the Frog* has added to Gary Paulsen's reputation as a first-rate writer of survival stories.

The Haymeadow

A great many of Gary Paulsen's protagonists are in their early teenage years, a time when young people often confront the world directly for the first time. Brian Robeson, for example, is 13 when he goes off to the woods in *Hatchet*, and David Alspeth is 14 when he sails off into the Pacific to scatter his Uncle Owen's ashes in the ocean.

Another 14-year-old protagonist, John Barron, appears in Paulsen's recent book *The Haymeadow*. As the story opens, in fact, it is early summer, and John has just had his fourteenth birthday the day before. He is disappointed that the birthday has come and gone so uneventfully, for he had wanted the new year in his life to bring change for him, and such change had not occurred. "He wasn't sure what he wanted to change," Paulsen tells us, "or how it should change, or even why it should change but he wanted something to change and nothing had and he felt cheated."[11]

John Barron lives with his father and the hired hands Cawley and Tinkner ("Tink") on the Three Bar S Ranch in western Wyoming. The ranch has been run by Barrons for generations, ever since John's great-grandfather, reputed to be "meaner than nine hells" but revered by John, had laid claim to its 960,000 acres and had made the claim stick using (as the legend told it) only his gun and two horses. While John's father still manages the ranch, however, it is now owned by an eastern corporation, which had taken it over after the old man had died. John's mother has also died, the result of being thrown by a horse, and so John lives alone with three grown men on the ranch, wanting now that he is 14 to be a man too.

John gets a chance to prove himself within days. Tinkner, the old hired hand, has been diagnosed with cancer, and John's father must stay with him at the hospital in town. It had been Tink's job, each spring, to take the ranch's 6,000 head of sheep up into a mountain pasture to graze for the summer, and now that Tink is unable to go, John learns that he will have to tend the sheep. At first this is more responsibility than John wants, and he proclaims to Cawley, "I ain't the one for this job" (*Haymeadow*, 38). But he has no choice in the matter, and so John and Cawley drive the sheep to the pasture, where John will stay alone for three months in a camp wagon with only two horses, four sheep dogs, and 6,000 sheep for company.

The final two-thirds of *The Haymeadow* tells of John Barron's adventures as he tends the sheep throughout the summer, and it is here that the book takes on many of the features of Paulsen's other survival stories. A boy alone in a natural setting, unknowledgeable about and inexperienced in that environment, must survive for months using only his own wits, and he must ensure the survival of a massive herd of sheep.

As soon as Cawley has ridden out of the valley, the story takes on the typical rapid pace of a Paulsen survival tale. Hearing one of the dogs barking excitedly, John rides into the herd, only to discover that a rattlesnake has attacked a sheep and threatens others. No sooner has he killed the rattler than a skunk menaces John and his horse, spraying them with its foul scent. As John is trying to wash the smell out of his hair and eyes, he hears the yelp of Pete, another of the dogs, and finds that the animal has severely lacerated the pad on one of its paws. While bandaging Pete's foot, he hears the high-pitched scream of a bobcat threatening the herd, and almost before he can react he is stampeded by 6,000 terrified sheep. John ends his first day in the haymeadow with his camp in a shambles and one of his dogs injured, filled with the feeling that he is totally incompetent at dispatching his duties—that he has no control over anything and will certainly never be able to survive three months of such crises.

Over the ensuing days and weeks, John survives many other catastrophes. A flash flood from a terrible thunderstorm carries his camp wagon into the nearby creek, and he has to spend days recovering all his gear. Night after night, he fights off coyotes that come out of the mountains to attack sheep at the edges of the herd, and he survives serious injuries to himself and one of his dogs by a bear. Through all this, John slowly accepts and then comes to enjoy the solitude of life in the haymeadow.

After 47 days alone, John sees a rider enter the valley one day and eventually realizes that it is his father who has come with additional supplies. John's father has been distant from his son, but here in the meadow they spend time getting acquainted. The father tells John stories about his mother and the true story of his great-grandfather's cruelty. No longer blindly worshipful of the old man, John Barron can finally hear the real reason that his ancestors lost the ranch—that much of the Barron family history derives from the old man's cruelty, not from his machismo. Listening to this man he has lived with but hardly known, John comes to enjoy his father's company, and the two decide to spend the remaining weeks tending the sheep together in the haymeadow.

Gary Paulsen reports that the idea for *The Haymeadow* came from the experiences of a friend who really did tend sheep in a Wyoming haymeadow over several summers. The boy really did have a particularly mean great-grandfather, and some details used in the story to describe the old man (for example, that he had once used a man's skull to make a button bowl) come directly from what was known about his friend's great-grandfather.

The survival episodes told in *The Haymeadow*, however, are Paulsen's own creations, and they resonate with experiences in his other adventure stories. Here, for example, a young boy has to learn to depend upon himself to survive, and in doing so he has to become closer to the natural environment that is both his dwelling place and a threat. Like Brian in both *Hatchet* and *The River*, John Barron becomes more accepting of his situation and better able to survive in a wilderness setting when he attends more carefully to the world around him. After several weeks in the valley, John realizes that his senses have been sharpened. "He had at first missed sound—" Paulsen tells us, "voices, talking, other people, but it wore away in some manner and now he didn't mind so much. Birds sang in the morning, the sound of the water running by in the creek was almost like music, and he found himself listening more, hearing more" (*Haymeadow*, 152). Also like Brian, John comes to be suspicious of the role of manmade implements in his survival. In *Hatchet*, when Brian finds a gun in the survival pack on the submerged plane, he is wary about using it and concerned about how it might cause him to start thinking that he is able to control the natural world rather than adapt to it. In *The Haymeadow* John does use a gun to ward off predators, but he has to re-evaluate its purpose after losing it in the flash flood and then finding it again. He remembers a comment that his father made—"A rifle is just a tool" (144)—to keep in perspective the function of this weapon in the natural world.

In *The Haymeadow*, writes a reviewer in *Publishers Weekly*, Gary Paulsen "writes with power and at times grace of the relationships between man and animal."[12] Certainly the novel adds to Paulsen's reputation as a talented writer about the outdoors.

Woodsong

Gary Paulsen has spoken often of the impact of the Iditarod dogsled race on his life and work. In the subtitle of his new adult work on the Iditarod, *Winterdance*, Paulsen refers to training for and running the race as a "fine madness." In interviews he has also called the experience "relentless" and "obsessive" and has claimed that the race becomes "so weirdly possessive of you that it ruins your life."

Although Gary Paulsen did not come to dogsled racing until he was in his forties, it is clear that the 22,000 miles that he has traveled behind a team of dogs has expanded and sharpened his awareness of the natural world. It is also likely that, without those experiences, Paulsen's natural adventure stories would not be nearly as gripping or authentic. And so it makes sense that *Woodsong*, which focuses on his dogsled experiences, fits neatly alongside the adventure-survival novels he has written.

Woodsong itself is not a novel, but rather an autobiographical nonfiction account of his early experiences in running dogs and of his first Iditarod race. Paulsen begins this collection of vignettes with the dramatic observation, "I understood almost nothing about the woods until it was nearly too late. And that is strange because my ignorance was based on knowledge" (*Woodsong*, 1), and then, through a suspenseful account of coming upon a deer being stalked by wolves, Paulsen reports that in this book he will share with us his new understanding, one that challenges the "fairy-tale version of the forest" (2) presented by Walt Disney and others.

In the book's first half, subtitled "Running," Gary Paulsen offers his readers a loosely assembled series of encounters with the animal and physical worlds while learning to run dogs in northern Minnesota. Some of these stories are familiar to Paulsen followers because he has told them elsewhere. His description of the beautiful and affecting run across Clear Water Lake related in chapter 2, for example, also appears in his adult book on dogsledding, *Winterdance,* and forms the plotline for the picture book *Dogteam* on which he collaborated with his wife Ruth. All the stories in *Woodsong,* however, are freshened by Paulsen's inclusion of vivid details and by his overarching purpose to present the natural world on its own terms.

Much of what Paulsen learns about nature is taught to him by his dogs. Sled dogs are often themselves still half-wild, Paulsen explains, and in retelling his experiences with them he again and again makes the point, as he did in a Trumpet Book Club video interview, that because they "have probably not changed in a thousand years," the dogs give him an opportunity to experience a "primitive point of view." In *Woodsong* Paulsen learns loyalty from his dogs, and courage, and even humor. In one entertaining episode, he tells of a game the dog Columbia would play with his fellow runner Olaf. Chained near him in the kennel yard, Columbia would push a bone toward the always eager and hungry Olaf and then stop while it was still just out of Olaf's reach, driving the simpleminded dog nearly crazy with frustration while Columbia, Paulsen swears, laughed and walked away. Coming to respect his dogs' intelligence, Paulsen learns to respect all animals, and shortly thereafter he decides to give up trapping and hunting because he can no longer justify the killing of any of nature's magnificent creatures.

The second half of *Woodsong* takes on a more rapid pace as Paulsen retells, through daily diary entries (based on a journal Paulsen actually kept during the race), the experiences of running his first Iditarod in 1983. Again, humor enters the story, especially in the comical race start during which Paulsen is pulled off the course and all through the city of Anchorage by his overeager team, and in his hallucination that a man in charge of federal educational grants and wearing horn-rimmed glasses and a trench coat—"the most boring human being I have ever met" (97)—has hopped onto his sled on the second day of the race. Paulsen's account is also in places highly dramatic. He tells of the dangers of crossing mountain ranges and an area called The

Burn that has been ravaged by forest fires, of the wind and bitter cold of the run up the Yukon River, of sleep deprivation and hunger, of great beauty and the trancelike "whiffling" of the dogs as they silently run, and finally of the run across a bay on the Bering Sea to within sight of the village of Nome, where the race ends, at which point Paulsen suddenly stops his team (and, in the book, stops his narrative account) because the Iditarod seems to be "not something that can be done. And yet you do it and then it becomes something you don't want to end—ever. You want the race, the exaltation, the joy and beauty of it to go on and on" (131–32). The tale of Paulsen's 17 days of racing makes for gripping reading, so that the reader, too, does not want the story to end.

At one point during the twelfth day of the race, Gary Paulsen records a transformation he has undergone: "I have changed, have moved back in time, have entered an altered state, a primitive state. At one point there is a long uphill grade—over a mile— and I lope alongside the sled easily, lightly, pushing gently to help the dogs. My rhythm, my movement, is the same as the dogs. We have the same flow across the tundra and I know then we will finish" (122). This transformation—of Paulsen becoming more like the dogs, more in touch with the natural forces around him—is identical to the change Brian reports having in *Hatchet* and David has in *The Voyage of the Frog* when both boys become acclimated to, and alive in, the natural world. For Paulsen himself, as for his characters, survival in the wilderness depends on adjusting oneself to that world rather than the world to the self. It depends on one's ability to change his or her view of the world, to meet nature on its own terms, and to move past a romanticized view of forests and animals.

Because there is no created character at the center of *Woodsong*—because the book, in other words, is about Paulsen himself—the story takes on a certain honesty that enriches Paulsen's collected survival stories. Certainly, the experiences of Brian Robeson, David Alspeth, and John Barron are not romanticized in their respective books, but the reader's awareness that these are created stories diffuses a bit their real-world impact. In

Woodsong, however, Paulsen is openly honest with his readers and himself. As he begins to run dogs, for example, Paulsen admits that he was "so ignorant, so steeped in not knowing, that I did not even know what I didn't know" (11). This straightforward confession authenticates the information and convictions that come later in the book. In an era of environmental awareness, when it has become fashionable to sing praises to the natural world, such honest statements enable Gary Paulsen to become something other than just another follower of the trend. Perhaps the only other author writing for young adults with such authenticity is Farley Mowat, who in books like *Never Cry Wolf* forcefully (and also with self-deprecating humor) argues for the need to examine and respect the animal world on its own terms. In *Woodsong*, Gary Paulsen's experiences in the wilderness give his passion for that world a similar energy, and his stories about wilderness survival take on a thematic force that goes beyond the simple person-versus-nature formula of most adventure books. Simply put, Paulsen's survival stories are songs not only for the survival of the self within a natural world, but also for the survival of that world itself.

Other Songs of the Earth

Because so much of Gary Paulsen's life has been spent in the outdoors, it is not surprising to find survival plots and subplots in many of his other works for young adults. In Paulsen's first Newbery Honor Book, *Dogsong*, for example, a 14-year-old Eskimo named Russel Suskit has become increasingly frustrated with the Westernization of his small village. He goes to learn the "old ways" from the village shaman, Oogruk, who teaches him to hunt and fish using primitive Eskimo weapons, to run a dogsled (the village is now using snowmobiles almost exclusively), and to search for the "song" within him that expresses his Eskimo identity. When Oogruk dies, Russel leaves the village and heads north in his dogsled on a "dreamrun" of personal survival and self-fulfillment, and at this point the novel takes on characteristics of Paulsen's other adventure books. Remembering bits of what Oogruk had taught him, Russel learns to hunt caribou, survive blinding snowstorms, and above all, care for his dogs. In a dream episode that takes him back to his primitive ancestors, Russel hunts a woolly mammoth, not for purposes of conquest, but so that he might take its meat back to his village and family, who are slowly starving. The survival episode ends similarly to Paulsen's adventure novels, with the protagonist having grown and become whole as a result of his struggles.

The novels *Tracker* and *The Foxman* also make use of vivid natural settings and survival subplots. In the former, the protagonist John Borne sets off on the opening day of hunting season to "take meat" by shooting a deer. With thoughts of his dying grandfather running through his head, however, he cannot bring himself to shoot the doe he finds. Instead, he decides to follow the animal to learn more about it, and ultimately to track the frightened doe until he is able to touch it. Through two nights and a day, John follows the deer through swamps and forests on a journey of survival and fulfillment. His survival, and ultimately the deer's, results from his coming to understand and be "at one"[13] with the animal.

In *The Foxman* an unnamed protagonist and his cousin Carl come upon a hermit living deep in the woods of northern Minnesota. The Foxman, who has been disfigured by a war injury, takes the boys in during bad weather, and slowly the three strike up an odd friendship. After Carl falls in love with a girl on a neighboring farm, the narrator continues to visit the Foxman on his own, and on one visit he is caught suddenly in a blinding snowstorm. The boy develops snow blindness, becomes disoriented, and eventually collapses under a tree in exhaustion, ready to accept his death, until the Foxman is able to track him down and rescue him. This survival episode becomes critical to the story's climax in that it contributes ultimately to the death of the Foxman.

Paulsen's autobiographical story *The Cookcamp* also contains a few survival elements, but here the protagonist's young age (he is five) creates a sense of wonder over the natural world rather than fear for its dangers. When the young boy, Paulsen himself, is sent to live with his grandmother in the woods of northern

Minnesota, he sees for the first time the marvels of forest life. Traveling through the deep forests, he is awed by the size and majesty of the trees that crowd in on the road. Dropping bits of food outside the cook trailer, he is fascinated by the chipmunks who boldly come to feed. Although at all times the young boy is protected by either his grandmother or the huge men working on the road crew she cooks for, his story becomes a kind of survival tale, and the wilderness setting takes on the same active role it does in his other works of adventure.

Some of Gary Paulsen's early books add insight to any study of his songs of the earth. In 1976 Paulsen published two books in a *Real Animals* series, with the subtitles *The Small Ones* and *The Grass Eaters*, about the wild animals of the American north woods. In the preface used in both books, Paulsen argues that animals have been analyzed to death by scientists and romanticized in films and on television. The purpose of these books, he explains, is "to take the animal out of his man-made 'eco-system,' likewise remove him from the 'cutesy' film industry, and put him back in the woods. Where he belongs, where he deserves to be, and where he can continue to be what he is in the first place. A *Real Animal*."[14] [Ironically, four years later Paulsen co-wrote with Art Browne Jr. a book about animals in the film industry entitled *TV and Movie Animals*. While Paulsen today might want to forget this study of the likes of Flipper, Lassie, and the animals of the Tarzan series, even then his attempts to see these animals on their own terms was apparent. Animal actors, Browne and Paulsen argue, retain their true animal traits, the result being that filming animals can be highly unpredictable.[15]]

The respect for the animal world apparent in Paulsen's survival stories surfaces also in the *Real Animals* books. Rabbits and foxes are shown to be highly intelligent, and deer are praised for their extraordinary survival instincts. The books are quite readable as informational animal books go, almost certainly because Paulsen intersperses his expository discussion of each animal with lively vignettes based on his own experiences in the woods. In a sense, *The Grass Eaters* and *The Small Ones* have the feel of Paulsen's later *Woodsong*—a tone created by his careful observation of natural occurrences and his introspection into the significance of those events.

In an interview by Marguerite Feitlowitz for *Authors and Artists for Young Adults*, Gary Paulsen reflected on the impact of the Iditarod on the mushers who run it. "The Iditarod may sound like a macho thrill," he explained, "but it's the opposite. You go where death goes, and death doesn't give a damn about macho. . . . Here's something that was brought home to me: macho is a lie. . . . Core toughness and compassion are the opposite of macho. The absence of fear comes with knowledge, not strength or bravura" (170). Indeed, the same philosophy might be said to inform Paulsen's stories of survival and adventure. In them, young protagonists struggle in the natural world and ultimately survive not because of macho strength, but because of intelligence and sensitivity. It is finally this twist on the conventional person-against-nature story that distinguishes Gary Paulsen's contribution to the genre.

4. Becoming Whole: Paulsen's Novels of Maturation and Growth

In their comprehensive study of the field of young adult literature, *Literature for Today's Young Adults*, Alleen Pace Nilsen and Kenneth L. Donelson remind us that "the *raison d'etre* for adolescent literature is to tell a story about making the passage from childhood to adulthood."[1] Because the teenage years are years of transition, it is not surprising that the literature written for and about young people will have, as its primary theme, the struggle to come of age. The classic and defining works in the field remind us how dominant this theme is. Jerry Renault in Robert Cormier's *The Chocolate War* seeks to grow up by "daring to disturb the universe,"[2] and the same struggle to grow and emerge whole and mature occupies the attention of Ponyboy Curtis in S. E. Hinton's *The Outsiders*, John and Lorraine in Paul Zindel's *The Pigman*, Alfred Brooks in Robert Lipsyte's *The Contender*, and literally hundreds of other characters in hundreds of other young adult novels.

Gary Paulsen, too, is concerned with the growth and development of his young protagonists, and a great many of his novels dramatize struggles to grow up by understanding self and world better. To Paulsen, the process of coming of age is largely a process of becoming whole, of coming to know and accept the self—of understanding the harmonies of life and living in concert with those harmonies. Paulsen's coming-of-age protagonists, at the end of their struggles, have learned to like themselves. They know the world better and delight in the connections between self, society, and the natural world. An examination of several of Paulsen's coming-of-age novels will reveal the various ways in which his characters struggle to become whole.

The Island

Perhaps Gary Paulsen's most obvious coming-of-age story is also, in terms of narrative structure, one of his simplest. In fact, the plot of *The Island* is so simple that the novel has received much criticism for its slow pace. Edwin J. Kenney Jr., writing in the *New York Times Book Review*, describes the book as "essentially a meditative novel that subordinates, indeed practically stops, external action,"[3] while the *Bulletin of the Center for Children's Books* refers to the novel as being "heavily thematic and unrelieved by action."[4] To be sure, *The Island* is a novel thin in plot and heavily laden with theme, but it is also a book that, for the patient reader, delivers significant insights into Gary Paulsen's conception of what it means for a young person to come of age.

Fourteen-year-old Wil Neuton has just moved with his parents from Madison, Wisconsin, to a house in the woods outside the village of Pinewood in the northern part of the state. Wil appears to be a normal teenager, suspicious of change. In Madison he has friends, knows where the good music stores and fast food restaurants are, and knows how to get by in school. When his father asks him what he thinks of the planned move, Wil replies, "I've got to be totally honest, Dad—totally honest. I think my whole life is going down the toilet."[5]

What happens, however, is that Wil finds a totally new life in his new home. Wil is a cyclist, and riding his bike down a quiet country road, he comes upon a small lake with an island in the center. The setting captivates him, and when he takes an abandoned boat out to the island, even his way of talking changes. "See what I have found," he says. "An island all for myself." The narrator tells us that to Wil, the island felt "like home" (*Island*, 22).

Wil returns to the island day after day, and while there he begins to study closely the natural world around him. He sees a heron and after studying its moves for hours, first tries to replicate the moves, then writes about the bird and tries to draw it. Wil begins to camp out on the island overnight, and he continues his studies. He remembers his grandmother and writes about and sketches her. He studies an anthill and watches a turtle attack and devour a fish. Watching a mother loon and her chicks in the water, a scene he thinks is "perfect," Wil also begins to understand the meaning of this place for him: "It wasn't seeking perfection that brought him to the island. It was more a finding of peace, and he didn't know he needed peace. A finding of harmony—that was it, harmony" (34).

Wil spends much time on his own, but he also has made a new friend, Susan, who lives on a nearby farm. Susan visits Wil on the island, comes to appreciate what he is doing, and slowly starts to fall in love with him. Wil's parents also become curious about their son's strange attraction to this place, but they cannot understand it. They send a psychologist to the island to talk with Wil, and their relationship with their son becomes strained.

Eventually, a reporter hears of Wil's unusual retreat and comes out to interview him. Soon other reporters come also, and before long Wil realizes that the harmony he had found on the island, the solitude of the place, is disappearing. But he is able to salvage a great deal from the experience. Looking out across the lake one morning, he sees his father huddled behind a tree. The man has been there all night, and realizing the love he has for his father, Wil suddenly realizes how much he wants to know him better. "If I can learn a fish," he reasons, "I can learn my father" (200). And so Wil invites his father over to the island, and rowing across Will realizes how this will all end. "It was a high thought, a high and clean and keening thought, as clear as the song the loon made in the slash of moonlight that night on the lake. It would end only when they found a bigger island" (202).

Wil's retreat to his island, much like the retreat Henry David Thoreau made to Walden Pond, is not an attempt to escape from life but rather an effort to step back from it, to examine and understand its essential nature. Wil's studies enable him to learn things, but he also discovers that living is not only about knowledge. "Perhaps when I am grown I will not know anything," he writes in his journal. "Perhaps that is the way it works, the way it is with growing. When you grow, you start to unlearn things" (127).

Whether Wil's change is one of learning or unlearning, it is without a doubt a change toward maturation. Wil no longer accepts the surface images of things, and he no longer takes for granted people, relationships, even the world itself. Nor does he retreat from the world as an indictment of it. "I am not here because something out there is bad," he explains to the psychologist. "I'm here because something here is good" (185).

On Wil's island, he comes of age. Harmony is what he discovers there, the harmony of self to the world and of the unity of the self. Wil Neuton's coming of age is clearly a process of becoming whole.

Gary Paulsen acknowledges that the inspiration for Wil Neuton came from his own son Jim, who, Paulsen explains, had "mental islands" he would retreat to when he needed to think something through. The meditative comments that begin the book's chapters are things Jim would say. "I ripped him off," confesses Paulsen. Yet even if *The Island* is, in a sense, Jim's story, it is also an expression of Gary Paulsen's own view that introspection is necessary for anyone to become a whole and thoughtful human being.

Tiltawhirl John

"It was in the summer when I came onto being sixteen that I ran off and met Tiltawhirl John and learned all about life and sex and what it meant to be a man" (*T-John*, 9). So begins the story narrated by the unnamed protagonist in Gary Paulsen's 1977 novel *Tiltawhirl John*. After the narrator's parents die, he is sent to live with his Uncle Ernest and Aunt Florence Peterson on their wheat farm in North Dakota. The boy does not dislike his guardians, but when his uncle gives the youth 80 acres of his own land shortly after he arrives, the youth feels pushed into farming and fears that he will never have a chance to try some other kind of life. As a result, having heard that it would be easy to find work at the sugar beet farms in the western part of the state, he runs off as summer begins to make his fortune hoeing beets.

The boy quickly finds that hoeing sugar beets is backbreaking work. He also discovers that the owner of the farm, Karl Elsner, is cruel and dishonest. Elsner uses mostly illegal Mexican immigrants as his workers and, after hiring them, works them long hours—"from can to can't" (22), feeds them badly, beats them if they are lazy or rebellious, and refuses to pay them, all the while threatening to turn them in to authorities and have them deported to Mexico if they tell.

One day, after Elsner attacks and rapes a young migrant named Maria, the boy can stand no more. He cleaves Elsner's head open with a hoe and, thinking that he has killed the man, flees the farm. A few miles down the road, he is picked up by three carnival workers in their truck—Tiltawhirl John, his wife Wanda, and his brother Billy. The three hear his story and invite him to travel the carnival circuit with them, and he agrees.

The youth quickly adjusts himself to carnival life, and he learns to love it. He helps John run the Tiltawhirl, learning how to jerk the throttle so that change spills out of riders' pockets and the girls' skirts fly up. He shills for the side shows, helping to draw in customers for Wanda's saliva pit (where she performs a striptease) and Billy's geek show (where he pretends to be a wild man from New Guinea and bites chickens' heads off).

As the boy learns carny life, he also learns the carny view of life: that carnival people are different from "regular" people out in the world, who are "turkeys and toads"—dumb and worthless (64). He also learns the carny philosophy: that the "carny world" and the "turkey world" cannot be mixed, that one cannot live in both but has to choose between them. Feeling loved and accepted by John, Wanda, and Billy, the boy chooses: "I decided that all I wanted for the rest of my whole life was to be a carny" (106).

The carnival people also teach their new companion about growing up. When the boy complains about how hard his young life has been, Billy chides him for complaining: "That hand is dealt, and you lost. It's tough, but it happens. Throw it in and take a new deal—smooth out a little. You're walking freaked all the time" (94). When he shyly takes an interest in a carnival girl, John encourages him, but when he has a particularly passionate encounter with the girl, T-John also advises, "What happened tonight out there with Janet—it's part of living. Don't let it make you go crazy" (117).

The young boy's fascination with carnival life dies when one day a mean-looking man named Tucker, who has previously known Wanda and is T-John's archenemy, shows up. The two men draw knives to settle the old dispute between them, and after both are badly wounded, T-John stabs Tucker and kills him. As the police arrive, the boy is discovered to be a runaway, and the book ends as he is taken back to his uncle's farm.

Gary Paulsen acknowledges that *Tiltawhirl John* is based on a summer in his own life when he ran off to the Dakotas to hoe in the beet fields, had a fight with the overseer, and joined up with a real Tiltawhirl John, Wanda, and Billy on a traveling carnival. Despite the hard times of that summer, Gary Paulsen looks back on it fondly, summing it up with the comment, "It was a wonderful summer. It was great."

For Paulsen's young protagonist in *Tiltawhirl John*, however, the summer on the run has been not quite so great. "I didn't plan any of it," the boy confesses as he begins to tell the story of that summer, "and if you want to know the iron truth of it, if I *had* known what was coming I don't think I would have done it" (*T-John*, 9). As the song lyric states, "Growing up is hard to do," and for the youthful narrator of *Tiltawhirl John*, who in this eventful summer has seen "so much of the wrong side of people that I'm not sure I want to be a person" (9), the cost of maturity has been high. "In the end," he concludes, "it's like T-John said once: some people like thunder and some like the rain. . . . Going off to seek my fame and fortune was maybe like tasting the thunder, even though I'm a person who likes rain best" (126).

Dogsong

Dogsong, Gary Paulsen's first Newbery Honor Book, tells another kind of coming-of-age story. Russel Suskit, 14, lives in a remote Eskimo village on the Bering Sea. His mother has run off with a white trapper, and his father prays to Jesus as a way to control his drinking. Russel hears the snowmobiles race past his small government house and hates the sound. "I am not happy with myself," he thinks.[6]

At the suggestion of his father, Russel visits the old village shaman, Oogruk, who senses the boy's restlessness and takes him in. Oogruk is the last person in the village to know of the "old ways," and he tells Russel stories of how the Eskimos lived before the coming of the white man and the snowmachines. Russel also learns to hunt and fish in the old ways, and finally he learns how to run Oogruk's sled dogs, the only team left in the village.

Oogruk tells Russel that he must listen for and find his "song," the most complete and beautiful expression of himself that comes from knowing his cultural heritage. "You don't get songs," Oogruk explains, "you *are* a song" (*Dogsong*, 28). As Russel takes the dogs out on longer and longer runs, he begins to hear the songs of things, and he finds himself changing.

One day Russel takes Oogruk with him out on the ice, where the old man announces that it is his "time" and says to the boy, "There is a thing you must do now to become a man. You must not go home. . . . You must leave with the dogs. Run long and find yourself. . . . Run with the dogs and become what the dogs will help you become" (72).

Russel heads north with the team, and on the trip he begins to dream of another Eskimo, an ancient hunter who is undertaking a similar journey. As Russel hunts meat for himself and his dogs, he dreams of the man hunting a woolly mammoth. He learns of the man's fear and of his courage, and he hears the hunter sing in exultation over the success of the hunt. "And Russel felt all those songs inside his soul, felt them even as the man in the dream sang" (98).

As Russel Suskit reaches the Arctic Circle, he comes upon a pregnant girl who has left her village in shame. He takes her in and then, because she is starving, leaves to hunt food. When he can find none, he calls upon the ghost of Oogruk for help, but no help appears. Russel learns another lesson of growing up—that he is on his own now: "Whatever decision he made, when the light came back, it was *his* decision, just as going back to live the old way must have been *his* decision" (154–55).

Dogsong ends as Russel saves the girl and finishes his run. He has changed now, become at-one with his ancient culture and himself, and the evidence of his growth is the song he has created by the end of his "dreamrun"—a song in praise of the dogs, the hunt, the arctic wilderness, and Oogruk—a song of himself, his "dogsong."

According to Gary Paulsen, the idea for *Dogsong* came as the result of an incident that occurred in the running of his first Iditarod. "In a small village a kid came running up and grabbed my dogs," he reports, "and I was terrified that he was going to get torn up, because he started to turn with them, and they kind of turned in on themselves and they'll rip up whatever's in the middle. . . . So I grabbed the kid and held him up over my head. God, he was little. I thought he was five or six, but he probably was nine. I held him over my head and I said, 'What are you doing?' And he said, 'I want you to teach me about dogs.' I couldn't believe that an Eskimo kid up there on the Bering Sea would have to ask some white jerk from Minnesota about dogs. So anyway, the whole idea [for the book] came to me then."

In *Dogsong*, Paulsen turns the little boy's curiosity about dogs into a search more significant and profound. Russel does want to know about dogs, but he also needs to understand his culture and himself. To become something more than what he now is—to grow up, in other words—Russel must find a way, as Oogruk says, to "live well." When Russel finds his song, it means he has become whole, connected with who his people have been and who he can be.

While a few of *Dogsong*'s plot elements seem contrived (Russel's discovery of the girl alone on the ice near the Arctic Circle, for example), Paulsen's inspired writing holds this book together and makes matters of plot structure seem less critical. The cadences of Gary Paulsen's writing here are the cadences of a song. *Horn Book*'s description of *Dogsong* as "a moving and beautifully portrayed rite of passage"[7] accurately summarizes the impact of this lyrically written book.

Canyons

While Russel Suskit grows up in part through coming to understand his culture, Brennan Cole, the main character of *Canyons*, grows as he meets a culture not his own. Brennan, at 14, is a loner who spends hours running, not to get in shape or to make the track team, but "to be with himself."[8] When Brennan goes camping with his mother and others in a canyon not far from their El Paso home, he feels the presence of someone and hears a voice, and when he finds a skull with a bullet hole in the forehead, his awareness of that spirit presence intensifies.

The spirit that Brennan senses is that of Coyote Runs, whose skull has been found by Brennan. As we learn gradually throughout the first half of the book, Coyote Runs was a 14-year-old Apache who in 1864, as his initiation into manhood, was allowed to accompany his tribe's raiding party for the first time. The Apaches cross over into Mexico and steal horses successfully, but on the way back they are met by soldiers from nearby Fort Bliss. Coyote Runs and a young friend escape into a canyon, but they are followed and, after the friend is killed, Coyote Runs is caught hiding and is executed with a shot to the forehead.

Because Coyote Runs was not able to return to the sacred medicine place before his death, his spirit is forever trapped in the canyon, and it is this spirit that Brennan hears. Unsure of what to do, he takes the skull with him, and with the help of a sympathetic teacher, a pathologist, and a packet of information received from the Western Archives in Denver, he comes to understand what had happened to Coyote Runs 100 years earlier. He also realizes what he must do: return the skull to the sacred place among the canyons so that the young Apache's spirit is finally set free.

With his mother becoming concerned and authorities closing in (Brennan has removed the skull from federal land illegally), Brennan sets off on a run across the desert to return the skull, his own journey into manhood. After evading the officers and getting help from his mother (despite her worry over his odd behavior), Brennan manages to locate the sacred place and set Coyote Runs's skull upon it. Feeling the spirit leave, Brennan offers up a wish for Coyote Runs: "Be free. Be the sun and wind and desert and stone and plant and the dust, be free and all the things there are to be" (*Canyons*, 183).

In setting Coyote Runs's spirit free, Brennan Cole has freed himself also. In the middle of his quest to find the mystery of the Apache's spirit, Brennan is unsure of who he himself is, uttering at one moment, "I am not me" (121). But as he accepts the responsibility for the future of Coyote Runs's spirit, he assumes responsibility for his own future as well. Brennan's journey out of loneliness and an undirected life into accountability and concern for himself and his "spiritual mate" Coyote Runs is his rite of passage into manhood. Paulsen acknowledges here that coming of age means not only searching for one's own fulfillment, but also reaching out so that someone else might be fulfilled.

The setting of *Canyons* is one very familiar to Gary Paulsen. Dog Canyon and Horse Canyon are not far from his current New Mexico home and are in the area where he was stationed at the end of his tour in the Army. In fact, it was while in the Army, on a weekend leave camping trip in nearby canyons, that Gary Paulsen found a skull with a small hole in the forehead. Paulsen left the skull there, but 30 years later his memory of the artifact triggered the writing of *Canyons*, a novel of the merging of two different times and cultures, and of the coming of age of two different boys.

Tracker

One of the shattering experiences of life is witnessing the death of a loved one, and one of the marks of maturity is the ability to accept such a death. John Borne is 13, the grandfather he has lived with for nine years is dying, and John cannot accept that fact. John loves his grandfather Clay, and he has grown up doing everything with the man. Together they tend the small farm on the edge of the Minnesota woods that Clay has lived on all his life, and together they have hunted each fall, not for the sport of it, but to "make meat." And in sharing chores with his grandfather, John is also exposed to the old man's insights about life. "[Hunting] doesn't make you a man," Clay reminds his grandson. "It doesn't make you anything to kill. We make meat, that's all" (*Tracker*, 29).

This hunting season, however, Clay's cancer has spread too far to enable him to leave the farmhouse, and so John must hunt alone. The night before the hunt, while hauling manure to the pasture, John sees a beautiful deer, and even though the doe sees the boy, she does not bolt. Now, on the hunt, John makes his way across the swamp below the farm, and as he stands in a pine forest of great beauty, the sun glinting off the ice crystals on the boughs, he sees the doe again, the same doe.

John raises his gun to shoot, but then he cannot. For something of such great beauty to die is wrong, he reasons, just as it is wrong for the grandfather he loves to die, and so instead of shooting he follows the doe.

Through the long afternoon John Borne tracks the deer, and slowly his thoughts about the animal mix with his thoughts about his grandfather. Knowing that he cannot kill the deer but also that he somehow cannot leave it alone, the boy in his exhaustion decides that his goal will be to touch the animal and reasons that, in doing so, a profound purpose will be served. "And if I do that," he reasons, "if I can follow her and touch her without giving her death then death will be cheated" (72). And if death is cheated, he imagines, then his grandfather will live.

All throughout the day and night and into the next day, John tracks the beautiful doe. He becomes exhausted by the journey but so does the deer, and late in the second day, the deer winded and blown, John approaches her and touches her.

John heads back to the farm that night and finds his grandparents worried about where he has been. Unsure at first of what to say, he finally tells his grandfather what has happened. The old man is moved by what the boy has done. Crying, he says to his wife, "Ain't that something, Aggie? He walked one down. Ain't that something? I'll take that with me. That's something I'll just take with me" (88–89).

As John sits down to eat, exhausted and still unsure of what this experience has meant, two thoughts come to him: "The first was that his grandfather was going to die. He would die and there was nothing John could do about it. . . . And the second thing was that death was a part of it all, a part of living. It was awful, a taking of life, but it happened to all things. . . . Dying was just as much a part of Clay Borne as living" (89).

When he was a freshman in high school, Gary Paulsen actually did track a deer down and touch it. "It isn't really hard," Paulsen claims. "I think Native Americans did it all of the time. Deer stay alive with really short, fast bursts to get away from wolves, but on the long haul they don't have it. They're really short-winded."

Paulsen's reasons for tracking the animal, however, were not the same reasons John Borne has in *Tracker*. Feeling out of place among his peers, the young Gary thought that accomplishing such a feat would get him noticed, make him popular. Unfortunately, when he returned to brag about the accomplishment, no one believed him.

Paulsen's manipulation of his own experience in *Tracker* reveals that his concern in writing the book was for something more than his young protagonist's popularity. To grow to maturity, young people must grapple with the same troubling issues that adults do, and death is one of the most troubling of them all. (In fact, as Gary Paulsen was writing *Tracker*, he was witnessing the death of his wife Ruth's father to cancer. Paulsen remembers his father-in-law as a "wonderful man" and acknowledges that the character Clay Borne is based on him.) In *Tracker* John Borne's struggle to understand and accept the death of a loved one is the struggle of many adolescents and adults alike, and his ability to come to terms with death represents his coming of age.

Whether it is John Borne handling death or Russel Suskit learning the melodies of life, Gary Paulsen demonstrates with them and with his other young characters how important it is that adolescents come to assume the challenges and responsibilities of adulthood. Taken as a whole, his coming-of-age stories are distinguished by believable young protagonists, significant maturation experiences, and thoughtful thematic lessons about both the challenges and the promises of growing up.

5. Uncle, Teacher, Soldier: Paulsen's Mentor Stories

In an article discussing adult characters in fiction for adolescents, young adult author Carolyn Meyer notes the vital role played in such works by what she calls "wiseguides"—concerned, instructive adults who are "directly involved in helping the main character in her or his progress toward maturity."[1] Certainly, mentors are as important to young characters in books as they are to teens in real life, and they are likely to appear in any work in which an adolescent struggles to come to terms with a new experience or idea.

The influential adult has a vital role to play in Gary Paulsen's novels, and nearly all of his stories contain such a character. Paulsen, in fact, seems to have a particular interest in mentors who guide the adolescent toward adulthood. Some of these helpful adults guide by counsel and advice, some by example, and some even influence young protagonists by counterexample—as sympathetic but broken figures who seek to ensure that a new generation will grow up without the same mistakes and tragedies that they have lived through.

Certainly, all of the books in which these mentor figures appear are also coming-of-age stories. But in some of Paulsen's novels the adult guide receives so much attention and figures so centrally in the story's plot that the book may seem, on one level, to be about him or her. When this happens, the novel takes on some of the feel of an extended character study.

There are several clues in Paulsen's work that reveal where his focus is—whether on protagonist or adult mentor, but the most obvious of these is that Paulsen frequently gives us this information directly. The coming-of-age novel *Tiltawhirl John*, for example, contains a very visible mentor figure in the carnival worker whose nickname is the title of the book, but from the opening sentence it is clear that this is a book about a young protagonist, not about John, his mentor. "It was in the summer when I came onto being sixteen," the narrator begins, "that I ran off and met Tiltawhirl John and learned all about life and sex and what it meant to be a man" (*T-John*, 9). The focus, from the outset, is on the young boy and his maturation experiences, not on the man who influenced him along the way.

By contrast, *Winterkill*, also clearly a coming-of-age story, is so preoccupied with the protagonist's mentor, Duda, that often the young boy forgets to talk about himself and what he learned and discusses Duda instead. At the very end of the book, for example, after Duda has been killed, the boy expresses his grief, but he does not reflect on the significance of the experience for himself. Instead he ends his account with the line, "and that's the story of Duda."[2] Without a doubt, this has, to a large extent, been Duda's story all along.

In his books about helpful and sympathetic adults, Gary Paulsen offers readers three distinctly different types of mentors. The first is the loving relative, who guides by advice and example. Second is the concerned teacher who selflessly aims to pass along important information or insights to the next generation. Finally, there is the broken warrior, one who has known the hard edges of life and who tries to steer a young protagonist away from that hardness or guide him or her through it. Uncle, teacher, soldier—all merit examination as important mentor types in Gary Paulsen's novels for young adults.

Uncles and Others: The Kindness of Relations

As Gary Paulsen has acknowledged, his parents' alcoholism motivated him, in his teenage years, to leave home as often as possible and to take up residence for weeks or months at a time with sympathetic relatives. Given that personal history, it makes sense that his books are filled with relatives who take it upon themselves to guide young protagonists in need of comfort and counsel. In general, these mentor figures are wise, sympathetic, and warmhearted. Serving sometimes almost as surrogate parents, they provide both emotional and physical support, and they guide largely by example. Two particularly notable mentoring relatives are the character of Uncle David in *Popcorn Days and Buttermilk Nights* and the figure of Paulsen's own grandmother in the autobiographical story *The Cookcamp*.

Popcorn Days and Buttermilk Nights

This story opens as its protagonist Carly, who is 14, is sent by his mother from his Minneapolis home to spend the summer with uncles in the tiny (population 200) northern Minnesota farming town of Norsten. Carly, who has increasingly gotten into trouble for vandalism in Minneapolis, suspects that neither of his uncles will want him, and so he is suspicious when, in wandering about the small town, he meets his Uncle David Hansen at the blacksmith shop. David, he learns, is the village blacksmith, and after a long day of hard work he loads Carly and his belongings into a buckboard and takes the boy home to live with him.

Carly walks into a household wholly different from the one he has known. An only child, Carly must adjust to the confusion of living with seven cousins. Used to having lots of free time on his hands, he must adjust to the hard work and long hours of life on a farm. From the beginning, however, Carly is made to feel like one of the family. On his first night at the farm, even though it is summer, Uncle David gathers the family in the parlor to tell them a "winter story"—a tale usually told to the family to pass the long winter nights. The story Carly hears is a humorous legend about a lumberjack who plays a final practical joke on his friends at the time of his death, and the boy loves it. Shortly thereafter, he comes to realize that his Uncle David and Aunt Emily have taken time for the story so that Carly might come to feel at home, like one of the family.

Within weeks, Carly comes to find happiness on the farm. As David leaves for the blacksmith shop before dawn each morning, Carly and his cousins begin the chores, but later in the day they also find time for play. Carly spends most of his time with his cousin Tinker, and one day he and Tinker decide to play rodeo by attempting to ride the young calves in the pen near the barn. Carly goes first and finds the ride terrifying, and when he finally falls off the calf and hears Tinker and his other cousins laughing at what is, to them, a funny sight, his old rage comes to the surface. He attacks Tinker, punching him in the face. That night David talks to Carly and informs him that if he wishes to stay on the farm, he will have to come work with him at the blacksmith shop.

David tells Carly that he sees himself not as a blacksmith but as a mechanic, "because a mechanic is somebody who fixes things."[3] Before long, working long hours alongside his uncle, Carly begins to realize that David is fixing not only farm implements, but Carly as well. David teaches by example. In his hard work, sensitivity to others and the world around him, and joy in living and laboring, David shows Carly another way to live, and Carly discovers one day that he has changed as a result of the experience. "There was a whole new feeling in me—" Carly explains, "not just a change but a whole new thing. I thought differently. I didn't think everybody was against me anymore—I didn't feel that the whole world had been designed just to dump garbage on my head, which I had come to believe for a time in the city. I was still fourteen, still caught in the same world, but there was something else now. I was . . . settled, somehow" (*Popcorn*, 69). As summer comes to an end and David and Carly have worked night and day to finish repairing farm machinery for the harvest, the family learns that a circus is stopping at a nearby town, and the children beg David and Emily to go. The family, however, has no money, and one night after David uncharacteristically gets roaring drunk at the town tavern (in part because he feels he has let his children down), the man hatches a plan to do something for all the children of the town. David and Carly return to the blacksmith shop, and day and night, without stop,

David begins to build his own carnival rides out of broken machinery in a field behind the shop.

In his exhausting work with David, Carly discovers that a close bond has formed between them. While making a circus seems a crazy thing to do, Carly jumps to the task because it is so important to David. "Something had happened between us," he observes, "something made of fire and steel, and if David was crazy by then, so was I" (92). In the experience, Carly also learns about joy. Looking up at his uncle one day, he notices a difference in his countenance: "his face was lighted somehow," and Carly realizes about David that in seeking to fulfill this dream for his family and his town, "he was just completely, totally, deeply happy" (95–96). As the story ends and David leads his children and the other townspeople to the circus, Carly realizes he has been given the satisfaction of a purposeful life. Sitting with a new girlfriend in the grass at the edge of the circus, aware of the gift David has given him, Carly talks "about what I wanted to be and do, and the circus went on and on" (100).

Gary Paulsen several times in his youth visited an uncle in northern Minnesota who was, in fact, a blacksmith and who did build circus rides for the kids in the town. Paulsen remembers riding in a grain wagon with him while his uncle, looking up at the puffy cumulus clouds that he said looked like popcorn, would sing over and over the line, "Popcorn days and buttermilk nights." For the young Paulsen, this relative was clearly a man of joy, one who communicated the satisfaction of clear intentions and hard work in all he did.

Popcorn Days and Buttermilk Nights tells the story of Carly's summer in Norsten, but in a larger sense it is the story of David, the kindly, gentle, joy-filled uncle who caused Carly to think differently, act differently, be different. The book is limited by its nostalgic, almost rhapsodic view of farm and small-town life (noticeable immediately in the opening portrait of the town of Norsten), but it does succeed as a portrait of a beneficent mentor uncle, "the blacksmith named David who could tame joy and hammer it into the shape of living, the way he hammered steel into the shape of a hoof" (*Popcorn*, 4).

The Cookcamp

If the Uncle Davids in Gary Paulsen's life gave him insight into life's challenges, it was surely his women relatives who provided the emotional support he rarely received at home. "I did have 'safety nets,'" he remarked in an interview several years ago, "all of them women. My grandmother and aunts were terribly important to me" ("SATA," 78). And so it is not surprising that at least one of these women, his grandmother, should appear in his books.

The Cookcamp is the autobiographical story of Paulsen's trip at age five to spend the summer with his grandmother, who worked as the cook for a crew digging a road through the northern Minnesota wilderness into Canada. It is wartime, 1944, and as Paulsen reports both at the beginning of the book and elsewhere, he is sent north because his father is fighting in Europe and his mother, bored and lonely, has taken in a lover and considers young Gary in the way.

The Cookcamp, despite being autobiographical, is told in third person, and it effectively captures the innocence, fear, and wonder of a small boy undertaking his first big journey into the world. Sent by train with a note pinned to his coat, the boy is watched over by porters as he travels north from Chicago, through Minneapolis, to a small town identified in the book as Pine, Minnesota (in actuality a location west of International Falls near the Canadian border). After a long wait, during which the boy swings his small legs while sitting on the huge station benches and watches the slow movement of the station wall clock, he is met by his grandmother and one of the large Scandinavian-American workmen (who seem to him like "big, polite bears" [28]) and taken to live in the cookcamp.

At the camp the boy spends his days learning to help his grandmother prepare food and set the table for the workmen (with the cups upside down, so the men will know they have not been used); feeds a chipmunk who lives under the cook trailer; plays with toy trucks in the dirt; and finally is permitted to ride with the workmen on their trucks, caterpillars, and graders for parts of each day. At night he sits on the men's laps while they play whist, pounding their cards upon the table, and is tucked in lovingly by his soft-spoken, nurturing grandmother. The story ends when the boy, who has become homesick and misses his mother, listens to his grandmother one last time as she tells him stories of her childhood and then is taken back to the train station for the long trip home.

Critics have given broad praise to *The Cookcamp*, calling it "a simply told story [that] strikes extraordinary emotional chords"[4] and "a beautifully written book"[5] and praising it for its "simplicity of story line and depth of imagery and emotion."[6] Writing in the *New York Times Book Review*, Patty Campbell acknowledges Paulsen's use of "the timeless, smooth-worn cadences of a folk tale" and praises the "almost unbearable poignancy" created in the little boy's story by the end of the novel.[7]

All of this praise acknowledges the skill with which Paulsen re-creates a small boy's sense of fear, need, wonder, and adventure, and the sensitive way in which the book chronicles the passing of those times of innocence and safety. But if it is the portrayals of childlike sweetness and curiosity that affect the book's readers, it is the character of the boy's grandmother that makes such feelings possible (and thus breathes life into the book) by nurturing and affirming her small, beloved grandson. Throughout the boy's escapades, the grandmother is everywhere—comforting him when he cries, singing him to sleep at night with Norwegian lullabies from her own childhood, bandaging his scrapes, and calling the boy, in a gesture of closeness and love, her "little thimble." By the end of the book, it has become clear to readers familiar with Paulsen's own life and work that one of his primary purposes in it is to pay tribute to his own loving grandmother, to capture her vitality, self-reliance, joy, and mother-love, and he does this not only in the actions of the story but also in a five-page "Portrait" of the woman that serves as an epilogue to the book.

In the "Portrait," which actually does tell the story of his maternal grandmother Alida Moen's life, Paulsen honors the woman for her courage, her perseverance in the face of her husband's and children's deaths, and for her loving guidance and devotion. The "Portrait" ends with an incident that actually happened when Gary Paulsen took his young son Jim up to meet his elderly great-grandmother. "She stole him," Paulsen writes, "completely and utterly with one piece of apple pie and a glass of milk,"[8] and what Paulsen says next shows without a doubt the continuing effect of this nurturing woman on him in adulthood: "And she looked up and smiled at him [the adult Paulsen], a smile that cut across all the years and made him wish he could sit in her lap—an intense, cutting longing" (*Cookcamp*, 115).

The grandmother in *The Cookcamp* is the only female mentor figure in Gary Paulsen's young adult works, and while she is clearly loved for her maternal instincts, there is something more to her virtue. In discussing his adult study of the female persona, a collection of vignettes entitled *The Madonna Stories*, Paulsen once commented, "Women are inevitably emotionally tougher than men. I want to understand their kind of toughness, and so feel that I must write about it" ("SATA," 82). While the softness of the grandmother in *The Cookcamp* is immediately apparent, her toughness in, for example, "straightening out" her daughter (the boy's mother) in letters throughout the summer shows that Paulsen sees in her an admirable courage and a determination to ensure that the right thing be done. It makes Paulsen's single female mentor something more than a one-dimensional figure, and it makes her a strong as well as loving example of the familial guide.

Other Relatives in Paulsen's Novels

Many of Gary Paulsen's other books for young adults also contain sympathetic, mentoring relatives. First there are the uncles: old Uncle David in *The Winter Room*, actually a great uncle or other distant relative, who tells the winter stories to Eldon and Wayne and their family and who teaches the two boys, through a remarkable act of physical strength and skill, that the old tales of superheroes are in some ways true and real; Uncle Owen in *The Voyage of the Frog*, who teaches his nephew David Alspeth to love sailing, the sea, and life itself; Uncle Harold in *The Foxman*, who takes in his nephew without question to save the boy from his alcoholic parents; and "distant Uncle" Knute, who does the same for his shirttail relative in *Harris and Me*. In *Tracker* it is a grandfather, Clay Borne, who raises and supports his grandson John, and who ultimately through his response to his own sickness teaches John to be as accepting of death as he is of life. And it is a grandfather who, in one of the vignettes in *Sentries*, helps Sue Oldhorn, a full-blood-ed Ojibway Indian, to understand and ultimately revere the old ways of her people. Clearly, blood relatives play an essential role in Gary Paulsen's works—as nurturing caregivers and loving guides.

Teachers: The Wisdom of the Knowing

Although Gary Paulsen sees his schooling as a disastrous part of his life, he acknowledges the influence of good teachers on him both in school settings and elsewhere. There was a high school teacher named Carlsen upon whom the science teacher John Homesly in *Canyons* is based, an individual who, according to Paulsen, "would grab a kid and save his ass. He didn't recognize adversity. . . . He'd make it happen; he'd crawl around out on the ground, whatever it took to do it." And there was the college English teacher named McMann at Bemidji State, who never lost faith in Paulsen and who came to congratulate him during a book signing at the very beginning of his writing career; and the drill sergeant named Gross who, during Paulsen's basic training, saw something worthwhile in the young man and helped to give his life a direction.

So, in his books, Gary Paulsen also gives us concerned, involved teachers. Whether they function within traditional classrooms or elsewhere, these teacher-mentors are all distinguished by their concern for their students, their passion for what they teach, and their determination to pass along what they know and believe to their young "pupils." John, the slave in the book *Nightjohn*, and Mick Strum, the artist in *The Monument*, are examples of such devoted yet nontraditional teachers.

Nightjohn

"This is a story about Nightjohn."[9] With that simple introduction
Sarny, a 12-year-old slave girl, begins her story of life on Clel
Waller's southern plantation in the 1850s, and of how that life
was changed when Waller one day brought into the yard a new
slave named John. Waller brought John in "bad," naked and
pulled along behind Waller's horse to teach him a lesson.
Immediately Sarny sees the whip scars that fill John's back, and
she knows that this is a slave who has created trouble for his previous masters.

Sarny lives in the slave quarters with Delie, a wet nurse who
has raised her since her birth mother was sold and whom Sarny
now calls "Mammy." Delie is cautious and teaches Sarny to be
so, but the very first night John moves into the dark, dirt-
floored slave quarters with them, Sarny sees evidence of the fire
that burns in John and discovers the flickering flame within herself. John wants a chew of tobacco, and he offers Sarny something in trade for it: "What I got to trade for a lip of tobacco is
letters. I knows letters. I'll trade A, B, and C for a lip of chew"
(*Nightjohn*, 34).

Sarny makes the trade out of curiosity, and quickly becomes so
fascinated with letters that John teaches her more. By the time
she has learned the alphabet up through H, she is also putting
words together, and in her eagerness she becomes careless and
spells the word "BAG" in the dirt within sight of her master.
Waller is outraged, accuses Delie of teaching the girl to read, and
punishes the woman, first by hanging her in chains all day and
then by stripping her, harnessing her to his wagon, and demanding a ride. When John can no longer stand the woman's abuse, he
confesses to teaching Sarny, for which he is punished with the
most brutal act in the book: having the middle toe on each foot
chopped off by Waller with a chisel and hammer.

As his wounds heal, John sneaks out one night and escapes
north (something Sarny learns he has done before). She is sad to
have lost him and the chance for learning, but then one night,
months later, she awakens to find him beside her in the hut.
Motioning Sarny to follow, John takes her off the plantation

down into some thick brush near the river, where, she discovers, he has set up a "pit school" to teach slave children to read and write and to which John will bring Sarny and the others night after night until their learning is complete.

Gary Paulsen came to write *Nightjohn* after years of doing research in original slave journals as part of an effort to write a biography of Sally Hemings, a slave who, as Paulsen says in the book's dedication to her, "was owned, raised, and subsequently used by Thomas Jefferson without benefit of ever drawing a single free breath" (7). As Paulsen found evidence of slaves who tried to teach slave children in pit schools, however, the story of these brave and most dangerous attempts to provide education captivated him. He created the character of Nightjohn out of various pictures and descriptions he came across, and the story of John's teaching emerged out of accounts in the slave journals. As Paulsen claims in a prefatory comment in the book, "Except for variations in time and character identification and placement, the events written in this story are true and actually happened" (39).

John is a talented, determined teacher, one driven to teach by a clear sense of what he is trying to accomplish. Early in Sarny's education, John explains to her that plantation owners punish slaves who try to become literate because "to know things, for us to know things, is bad for them. We get to wanting and when we get to wanting it's bad for them" (39). Later, as John tries to explain to a frightened Delie why he must teach and the children must learn, he articulates his reasons even more precisely. "They have to read and write," he tells Delie. "We all have to read and write so we can write about this—what they doing to us. It has to be written" (58). Significantly, Sarny not only begins to learn the alphabet, but she learns the purpose of her schooling as well. In a coda to the story that builds dramatically with a repetition of the phrase "Late he come walking," Sarny concludes her story with the sentence, "Late he come walking and it be Nightjohn and he bringing us the way to know" (92). Not knowledge, but the way to know—a commodity more valuable than knowledge itself.

In an extended review of *Nightjohn* in the *Wilson Library Bulletin*, Frances Bradburn acknowledges the risks Gary Paulsen has taken in writing this book. First, she points to the graphic violence in the story, including as it does references to beatings, rapes, castration, and mutilation by bloodthirsty dogs. Second, Bradburn mentions Paulsen's risk "as a white western author writing from the southern slave's perspective in what he perceives to be an African American dialect." Finally, however, she concludes that the risks are justified because the result is a story "that must be told if middle[-grade] readers are to begin to understand racially where we are as a nation today, the lengths we all have traveled, and the distance we have yet to go."[10] *Nightjohn* is a stark, bold story of the relationship between literacy and freedom, and as Sarny is taught by Nightjohn, so are we all.

The Monument

"Watch and learn and work and live and be,"[11] advises artist Mick Strum to Rachel Ellen ("Rocky") Turner after coming to her sleepy town of Bolton, Kansas. Clearly, his advice is that of a teacher, and Mick becomes Rocky's teacher in matters of both art and life.

Mick Strum has come to this small farming community at the invitation of town officials to construct a monument for Bolton's war dead. It seems that one of its residents, having seen the Vietnam Veterans War Memorial in Washington, D.C., thinks it would be good for the town to have its own memorial, and so Mick Strum is brought in to do the job.

In Mick, Bolton gets more than it bargained for. He whirls into town, sketching everything he sees—buildings, gravestones, even town residents. When those residents all gather at a town meeting to discuss the monument, Mick creates an uproar by displaying the drawings, some of which depict individuals in embarrassing ways—a respected female townsperson in the nude, another with money in her hand and a look of greed on her face. Mick repeats Katherine Anne Porter's observation that "Art is what you find when the ruins are cleared away" to the residents, and having made of the town a ruin, begins to discuss with them what sort of monument will "hurt and make you weep and lift you into love at the same time" (*Monument*, 130). After the meeting, Mick Strum sets about constructing a beauti- fully simple memorial on the courthouse lawn—an aisle of 18 trees, one for each fallen town veteran, with benches among them and a simple plaque at each tree naming one of the dead soldiers. His job finished, Mick Strum leaves town, having taught its residents about art and having made them aware of their own fears and hopes.

If Mick Strum is a good teacher to the people of Bolton, he is an even greater one to Rocky Turner, and she is much in need of such a mentor. Rocky, a mulatto with a lame left leg, is an aban- doned child who is finally adopted from the orphanage by Fred and Emma Turner, Bolton residents, who treat the girl kindly but also drink heavily and sometimes ignore the girl. Rocky has no friends except Python, the stray dog she has befriended, and so when she finds Mick drunk and sleeping upside down in his car on his first morning in Bolton, she is more curious than offended by him, and she begins to follow him about town.

Rocky is fascinated with Mick's view of the town and of his ability to draw affecting and accurate images of it. "The light," he exclaims while looking down the street. "See the light?" (56). After trying to sketch the light, he introduces himself to Rocky as Mick—"Just Mick. It doesn't matter. Names don't matter, do they? Only the light matters, the light and the way colors move in the light. That's all. And shapes. Line—it's all in the line" (57).

Before long Rocky, too, begins to draw, and Mick instructs her first by affirming what she already has within her. "Can you," Rocky asks, "teach me [to be an artist]?" and Mick replies, "No. Not to be an artist. You already are that—I knew you had the hot worm in you when I first saw you walking up to the station wagon. . . . But I can teach you something of technique, of line, of color" (83–84). Mick instructs Rocky as a typical teacher might. He gives her a book to read on Degas, assigns her pictures to sketch, and slowly shows her, by example, how to look closely and insightfully at what she draws. At the end of the book, after Mick has left town, Rocky (now signing her name as Rachel) writes him a letter to report on the town's reaction to its war monument. The letter ends as Rachel describes the touching scene of a fallen soldier's father sitting quietly under the tree bearing his son's name. "Maybe after a long time I will be able to draw it," Rachel writes. "I guess that's what makes an artist, isn't it?" (149). Rachel "Rocky" Turner has come to understand the significance of art, and with Mick's help, she is in the process of becoming the kind of artist she wants to be.

The story of how Gary Paulsen came to write *The Monument* reveals something of his intentions for the book.

"I have friends on the Black Wall [the Vietnam Veterans War Memorial in Washington]," he explains,

> and so when I was in Washington I thought, 'I'm going to go down and see it and I'm not going to be swayed by this crap. I'm going to be tough, and to make sure that I'm not bothered I won't go when other people are there because if somebody else is crying, it'll make me cry.' And so I went down there at four o'clock in the morning. It was summer, and I was the only one there, and it busted me up. I was on my hands and knees—just completely broken down. And as I was sitting there, this old woman, probably 70, comes out and she starts moving the things people had put along the wall. I just blew, and I told her, 'You can't touch that. What in the hell is the matter with you?' She was sweet, and she was crying. She said, 'I work for the park; I have to clean the wall. We clean it.' And she was moving stuff away so she could clean it. And she cried, and I asked her, 'Do you cry every time?' She said, 'Every day.'

At the end of the novel, Paulsen explains, "I wanted to show art, show how it can shake and crumble thinking; how it can bring joy and sadness at the same time; how it can own and be owned, sweep through lives and change them—how the beauty of it, the singular, sensual, ripping, breath-stopping, wondrous, frightening beauty of it can grow from even that ultimate ruin of all ruins: the filth of war" (*Monument*, 151). This is the view of art that Mick Strum gives to the people of Bolton, Kansas, and to Rocky. This is what, as a masterful and sensitive teacher, he causes them to learn.

Other Teachers

Other teachers appear in Gary Paulsen's books, although none perhaps so forceful and effective as Nightjohn or Mick Strum. In *Hatchet* Brian Robeson recalls Mr. Perpich, his English teacher, as he tries to take stock of his situation after crashing in the Canadian wilderness. "Get motivated," Brian remembers Mr. Perpich saying to his students. He also recalls this teacher preaching self-reliance, and he realizes the resource he has in himself as he recalls Mr. Perpich's exhortation, "*You* are your most valuable asset. Don't forget that. *You* are the best thing you have" (*Hatchet*, 51). In *Dogsong* the shaman Oogruk tells Russel about his ancient Eskimo heritage. He teaches the youth how to run a dogsled, hunt seals, and survive in the arctic wilderness. Oogruk also shows Russel how to find fulfillment by creating in himself a "song" of life.

Mr. Perpich and Oogruk, Nightjohn and Mick Strum—all contribute to young peoples' lives by teaching them to think and feel and know. All exemplify the kind of beneficent and caring teacher that Paulsen depicts as being vital to young peoples' development.

Soldiers: The Comfort of the Broken

In his hard and sometimes chaotic life, Gary Paulsen has seen and lived with many individuals who have been broken in some way by life's struggles, and his writing reveals his great compassion for those so unfortunate. Paulsen's attitude toward the downtrodden, however, goes far beyond pity, for he seems to see in them a kind of dignity, a wisdom and insight into the world from which all of us can learn. Paulsen's friend and former editor Richard Jackson says of Paulsen's life, "He had a really unstable, unhappy childhood with parents he couldn't rely on. Actually, in all of the books there is an imperfect older person upon whom the kid is dependent and who is worthy of that dependence. . . . That person comes as close to creating a good parent as Gary can do for himself" ("SFF," 9).

Whether Paulsen seeks to create good surrogate parents for his young characters or just adult companions for them, clearly the "imperfect elder" character serves an important guiding purpose in his stories. Often former soldiers who have witnessed the ravages of war, occasionally defeated battlers of other types, these broken warriors, world-weary and sometimes melancholy, have all seen something of the dark parts of life, and consciously or unconsciously they seek to shield children from the darkness, or guide them through it, or rescue them from it. Shattered or injured by life, these men (for these warriors are all male in Paulsen's books) are only occasionally cynical about it. Hardened by struggle, they are still in some ways fragile and vulnerable. The broken soldier adds a new dimension to Paulsen's collection of adult mentor figures.

Dancing Carl

One of the most elegantly simple of Gary Paulsen's books, *Dancing Carl* was first conceived of and designed as a ballet, and in the late 1970s, in fact, a seven-minute segment of it was performed by two dancers on Minnesota Public Television. The story is told by 12-year-old Marshall ("Marsh"), who with his friend Willy Taylor lives in McKinley, Minnesota. Shortly after Thanksgiving, as the small town is beginning to make plans to flood its two ice rinks, former resident Carl Wenstrom arrives back in town. Not a lot is known about Carl except that he had been a bomber pilot in World War II, had returned from the war a broken man and become a heavy drinker, and was now being cared for by the townspeople of McKinley.

As the rinks are flooded and skating again becomes the center of town life, Carl moves his few belongings into the warming house, tends the rinks, and particularly watches out for the young children who come to skate. Marsh and Willy are curious about this eccentric, gentle man, and later, when he starts to dance, they become fascinated by him.

Carl's dancing, actually a series of strange and graceful movements on the ice in street shoes, captivates the whole town, and although Marsh and Willy do not understand it, they begin to see how Carl becomes transformed by the dance: "like maybe he's got the shine on him or something."[12] One day, Marsh brings his model of a B-17 airplane to the warming house, thinking that Carl might like to see it because of his experiences in the war. Carl recoils at the sight of the model and begins to hallucinate with the horrors of what happened to him in such an airplane. As he crumples to the floor, Marsh and Willy fear that they have broken for good this fragile, strange man.

Shortly thereafter, an oddly dressed older woman by the name of Helen Swanson begins showing up at the rinks, and Carl is wholly captivated by her. His courtship, however, is most unconventional: day after day, as she comes to the rink, he dances for her, never saying a word. One day, he carries a rose out on the ice with him and, at the end of his dance, places it on the ice. After some hesitation, Helen moves to the rose, and Marsh tells what happens next: "She came across the ice and bent without seeming to bend and one hand came out of the muff and she picked up the rose—picked it up and looked at Carl, looked him right in the face, right in the eyes and she smiled and Carl answered the smile and we all breathed again" (*Dancing*, 104).

Dancing Carl is a most peculiar mentor figure: he is not shown to be particularly intelligent, is more in need of comfort than able to be a comforter, and seldom even speaks to the two boys who are so affected by his actions and behavior. But there is no mistaking Carl's effect on Marsh and Willy. As Marsh begins to tell his story, he sums up the man's impact by saying, "That winter Dancing Carl became everything at the rinks and taught us about living and being what we were and loving all mixed into the cold and ice-blue flat of the skating rinks" (7).

There is evidence throughout the book of Carl's "teaching." The boys realize early on that Carl has an enormous power to "make people do what he needed them to do" (42), and they see him using that power to protect the young and innocent. Carl saves the best bench in the warming house for the smallest children, and with the force of his stare alone, he drives a bully off the hockey rink. When Marsh and Willy ask Carl about how he learned to dance, he provides a worldview rather than an explanation, answering, "It's all movement—not a dance. Everything in life is a movement, a swirl, a spin. And the movements have color. Like some swirls are red and some are green and some are blue like the ice and they all mix together and everything in life is a movement of color to music" (68). To be sure, by the end of the winter, Marsh and Willy are changed by having known Carl, and by having seen him dance. So changed are they that, despite rumors about what has happened years later to Carl and Helen, they have seen in Carl, and learned from him, sweetness, love, and both the wonder and the poignancy of life. After all that has been rumored, Marsh concludes, "All that mattered then and all that matters now is that Helen stooped to pick up that rose" (105).

Dancing Carl is based on a real Carl whom Gary Paulsen knew when he was young, a World War II bomber pilot who, just like the character in the novel, bailed out of his B-17, fell alongside the plane for a few seconds, and saw his belly gunner trapped and on fire. "Normally the belly gunner would have carried a gun and shot himself," Paulsen explains, "but this guy had no handgun and he was trying to choke himself with his mike cord, kill himself because he was burning. And it drove Carl nuts. Carl spent a lot of time in a German prisoner of war camp too." The real Carl of Paulsen's youth returned to his small Minnesota town and did, in fact, tend the ice rinks while townspeople looked after him. And there was a real Helen, a woman Paulsen suspects was retarded. "And she looked just like that—that little tweed suit and little pillbox hat. . . . She was just the sweetest thing, and he just fell in love. Kripes, Carl danced all over for her."

After the book was published, Paulsen "got letters from towns all over Minnesota and Michigan and Wisconsin and North and South Dakota asking if I was writing about their Carl. Every town had a Carl—some guy who had been screwed up in the war and lived at the skating rink and took care of stuff for kids." While all of those real "Carls" may not have been mentors, the letters prove that each had a significant impact upon the people in his town and was remembered by them. Each was a broken warrior who, like the character in *Dancing Carl*, touched the lives of those around him.

The Night the White Deer Died

Billy Honcho, like Dancing Carl, is a town drunk, and like Carl, he comes to have a profound impact upon a young person in his town. Billy is 53, a full-blooded Pueblo Indian and former governor of his reservation. He now lives in the artist colony town of Tres Pinos, New Mexico, and spends his days in the town square, drinking wine and begging money from the tourists.

One day Billy catches the attention of 15-year-old Janet Carson, a loner who has lived in Tres Pinos for about a year with her divorced mother, who is a sculptor. Despite Billy's drunkenness, Janet sees the inner dignity of the man in the proud way he carries his shoulders, and she begins to seek him out in the town square, trying to get him away from alcohol and to sober him up. At times Billy tries to hustle money from her; at times he cooperates and sobers up at her urging. Unsure of her motivations, he asks Janet again and again, "Why are you here? Why have you come?"[13] And Janet herself is unsure.

Janet has been having a strange dream about a proud Indian warrior, dressed all in white, who goes out to hunt a white deer. In each repetition of the dream the warrior stalks the deer, draws an arrow, and shoots, but before the arrow reaches the deer, Janet awakens, cold and terribly afraid.

Janet does not understand the dream, but after befriending Billy for some time she begins to wonder whether he is, in fact, the dream warrior. At the same time, Billy begins to be fascinated by Janet. He brings her a beautiful Kachina doll, a figure used by Indians to instruct in the ways of the gods, and he chants for her and takes her to see the Indian pueblo he used to govern.

Then, one morning, Billy comes to Janet's house, dressed as a warrior all in white and riding a white horse. He takes Janet up into the mountains, where in a talk that is "half-music" and with movements that are "half-dancing," Billy tells Janet the history of his people, their struggles, glories, battles, and even-

tual humiliation and defeat. Listening to Billy, Janet comes to
love him.

> Not so much him, and it was not so much gushy love, but she
> loved what he was when he told the story, loved not just what
> he was but what he should have been, loved what he *could* have
> been if the time had been right for him.
>
> She loved him. Because he was the Indian in the dream, but
> he was more than that too; more than simply a dream person,
> because when he'd told the story of the battle, she had actually
> seen him change and become a warrior in the fight. (*Night*, 96)

After teaching Janet, Billy commands her to leave, explaining
that "it is time" for his life to end. "I have done most things
once," Billy explains. "It is no good to do things twice. Down
there [pointing to the town below] there is only the wine" (98).

What Janet has learned from Billy is the history of his people,
but she has also learned more. That night her dream returns,
and this time the deer kill that has haunted her is completed.
After seeing the ugliness of the dead animal, Janet turns in the
dream to accuse the warrior and finds him gone, and then the
white deer gone, and then the nightmare itself gone. Death fulfilled, even the death of something good and beautiful, is no
longer a horror. The nightmare comes from endlessly living that
death, from the anticipation of it.

The Night the White Deer Died is not one of Gary Paulsen's
better-known works, and the reviews it received were mixed.
One flaw of the book might be that the allegorical dream
sequences seem too unrealistically tied to actual events in
Janet's life as Billy becomes identified with the dream warrior.
Another might be that the close relationship, even love, that
forms between a teenager and a 53-year-old man seems too
incredible to believe (despite Paulsen's revelation that the story
is based upon a real relationship of that type that he witnessed
while living in Taos). Still, *The Night the White Deer Died* generates real feeling, partly because of Paulsen's dramatic pacing of
the story, partly because of his attention to precise and vivid
detail. In addition, the novel presents us with another broken

yet dignified teacher-warrior, a character who evokes both sympathy and a sense of honor.

The Foxman

In his 1976 nonfiction book *The Grass Eaters*, Gary Paulsen reveals that much of his early knowledge of the "grass eaters" of the northern forests—deer, moose, and fox—came from knowing in his youth an expert trapper who lived as a hermit in the woods of northern Minnesota, a man the young Gary Paulsen and his cousins and friends called "The Foxman." The Foxman was a former soldier who had been horribly disfigured by chemical gas during World War I. "It ate the entire lower part of his face off," Paulsen remembers, "and they healed it with grafts and stuff, but the grafts didn't take, so it was this huge kind of callous, and all of his teeth showed. There were no lips left; he was really quite ugly. Anyway, he did exist, and we'd go to a shack and talk to him and stuff. He played the guitar; he was really a neat guy."

The real Foxman of Gary Paulsen's youth is the basis for yet another of his fictional mentor-soldiers. In the 1978 novel *The Foxman* an unnamed 15-year-old narrator, abused by his parents during their alcoholic binges, is removed from his home by a judge and sent to live with his Uncle Harold and Aunt Margaret Peterson on a small farm in the woods of northern Minnesota. At first homesick and lonely, the boy slowly comes to love life on the farm, and he spends the next two years there. "It seems like one minute I was still new at the farm, in the woods," the boy recalls after several months with the Petersons, "and the next it was like I'd never been anywhere else."[14]

The narrator's best friend and companion on the farm is his cousin Carl, a boy almost his age and one knowledgeable about farm and woods life. Carl and the narrator work and play together—leading a horse team to "buck" stumps in order to clear a new field for planting, for example, and making cross-country skis to use while hunting and trapping in the woods throughout the winter.

On one winter trip into the woods, the two boys travel much farther north than they have ever been while tracking a fox, and as a severe snowstorm threatens, they look for shelter and happen upon a tar-paper shack hidden in the woods. The shack is the home of a hermit trapper who has a horribly disfigured face but who nevertheless takes them in and saves them from the storm. Learning the next morning that this hermit is a skilled trapper, the boys give him the nickname "the Foxman" as they leave.

Over the next several weeks, as Carl becomes infatuated with neighbor and first-girlfriend Bonnie Anderson, the narrator finds himself often returning alone to the woods. Having come to feel at home there, the boy retreats to the woods because of their beauty and solitude, but he also finds himself, week after week, making his way to the Foxman's shack. The boy is curious about this gentle, disfigured recluse, but he is uncertain about what brings him back again and again to see the man. After the Foxman thanks him for returning on his second visit, the boy realizes that his motives are not simply altruistic—that "I came for me, more than for him, because he had something I wanted, only I didn't know what it was" (*Foxman*, 76–77).

In short, what the narrator discovers is that he is coming to depend on the Foxman for advice and companionship—that the man is "taking over where my folks left off when they started drinking years before." He begins to trust the Foxman with his questions about life and growing up, and the boy is comforted to find that the man "always gave me an answer I could live with and which usually turned out to be right, or at least got me on the right track, and that's a kind of love. Having somebody do that for you" (98).

The Foxman's mentoring of his 15-year-old charge extends over two months, during which the youth visits the recluse every weekend. The boy learns a great deal about the woods from the old man, particularly about how to trap foxes by taking advantage of their innate intelligence and "out-foxing" them. He also brings his schoolwork with him to the Foxman's shack, and he uses the man's extensive library and broad personal knowledge to extend his learning. In particular, the youth remembers the Foxman teaching him "to question things and make sure they were right before accepting them" and to "always ask the second question"—not just to "ask why, but why why?" (92).

In addition, as any good mentor would, the Foxman helps the boy to resolve personal problems. One matter in particular that has been vexing the youth is the laughter that accompanies grim stories of World War I told by his Uncle Harold's father Hans and Uncle Agile in the Peterson living room each winter night. The laughter seems particularly inappropriate to the boy now that he has come to know the Foxman, who was so badly disfigured in that same war, and he asks the Foxman to explain what might motivate men to laugh about such a horrible experience. "All they're trying to do is pluck a rose from manure," the Foxman explains. "The men telling those stories are only trying to remember some of the parts of the war that might be worth remembering—trying to find some use in all that waste" (87).

The Foxman is resolved in the same way as *The Night the White Deer Died* and many of Paulsen's other mentor stories: the death of the mentor. After the boy is blinded by the bright sun on the snow and then is caught in a storm on a trip to the Foxman's shack, he is rescued by the Foxman, but the old man has developed the deep cough of one seriously ill from overexposure to the severe cold. Returning to the shack a few days later, the boy finds the Foxman near death. The old man, in a final act of mentorship, offers his books and hides to the boy but also makes one last request—that his shack be burned with his body in it in order that no trace of him be found. Taking only a single fox pelt, the boy honors the Foxman's last wish, and the book ends with the youth reflecting that the pelt's "beautiful fur, red and rich and deep, [was] almost as beautiful as the Foxman" (119).

While praising the characterization and vivid settings of *The Foxman*, a reviewer writing in the *Bulletin of the Center for Children's Books* was mildly critical of Paulsen for having "created a situation more than a story."[15] The objection has some merit, for once the Foxman is introduced nearly halfway through the book, the narrator's struggle to grow up becomes almost totally subsumed in portraiture of the Foxman and attention to the odd friendship that develops between man and boy. Still, the sympathy Paulsen evokes for his reclusive warrior-mentor generates its own energy in the novel, and Paulsen's narrator writes the story at 17, looking back at what had happened to him two years earlier, which gives the book a reflective quality that implies a great deal about how the Foxman, as mentor, has enabled the narrator to grow up. *The Foxman* may, indeed, seem to be little more than an extended character study at times, but even vivid character studies can provide memorable reading experiences.

Winterkill and *The Crossing*

While the Foxman, Billy Honcho, and Carl Wenstrom all remain unchanged as they influence young protagonists through their passionate and fragile struggles with life, a few of Gary Paulsen's mentor-warriors go through dynamic changes, or at least begin to undergo such change during the course of their stories. These figures, too, enter the lives of boys in need of guidance, and in the course of the novels they begin to lose some of their cynicism and hardness as they act positively to help others. Two such characters are Duda from Paulsen's early novel *Winterkill* and Sergeant Robert Locke from his acclaimed book *The Crossing*. Because there are so many interesting parallels between these world-weary battlers, they are best examined together.

Duda, a former soldier, is a new police officer in the town of Twin Forks, Minnesota, and when the unnamed 13-year-old narrator of *Winterkill* first meets him, the boy has been illegally fishing for walleye in a river at the edge of town. The boy is frightened immediately by the tough-looking officer, and within minutes he realizes that he has a reason to be afraid. Duda forces the boy to reveal his illegal catch, calls him "you little puke," tells him to gut and clean the largest walleye, and then takes the fish for himself, saying as he leaves, "And that, punk kid, is your introduction to graft" (*Winterkill*, 16).

After the boy's parents, who drink and fight all the time, actually hurt him in a confrontation, he is taken to live at a series of foster homes, and during this time Duda, still the tough cop, begins to watch out for the teen. After the narrator's parents sober up and bring him home, the boy once more gets into trouble by breaking into a neighbor's garage, and once again Duda punishes him severely by driving him 10 miles out of town and, in 10-below weather, making the boy walk back home.

Despite this tough love, the boy starts becoming attached to Duda, and he starts riding with him on his nightly patrols. The two spend hours talking about the town and the people in it and about hunting and fishing, and slowly the boy begins to think of Duda as the father he has always wanted.

All this changes during two of Duda's patrols, however. First, he manages to stop two out-of-town bank robbers on an isolated road outside of town. Even though the robbers surrender and begin to step out of their car, Duda's hardened war persona has clicked in, and with almost no hesitation he fires his rifle, killing the robbers in cold blood (an act witnessed only by the horrified boy). Later, after the man and boy have become reconciled and Duda is considering adopting the teen, the boy is with him again when the officer stops an armed teenager. Stepping out of the patrol car, Duda's body "arched and his gut disappeared like a bullfighter, like he did the night of the bank robbers, and I thought man, he's doing it again, turning into whatever it is he was on that night" (140). This is a changed Duda, however, a man who has come to love the boy and has come to feel that his life has a future. As a result, Duda drops his guard, and when the frightened teen runaway raises his gun toward the officer, Duda is defenseless, because he "had put the walls down and wasn't ready, wasn't ready, wasn't ready" (141). The gun sounds, Duda is mortally wounded, and the story's narrator is left to mourn the loss of this complex mentor and friend—a man who at first was too hardened to live, and then became too softened to survive.

A similar change in a mentor-soldier occurs in *The Crossing*. Sergeant Robert Locke, stationed at Fort Bliss near the Texas-Mexico border, is "above all things, a sergeant."[16] Locke, that is, looks like a soldier, acts with the military discipline of one, and carries the steely gaze of the combatant wherever he goes. Where he frequently does go is across the border to Juarez, and once there, night after night, he drinks himself into numbness so that the faces of his former soldier friends, the ones who have died in combat, do not reappear before him.

Manny Bustos lives in Juarez. A street urchin abandoned by his mother, 13 or 14 years old, Manny scurries about the streets of Juarez, begging for food and coins from the American visitors and trying to stay hidden from the street bullies who chase and attack him. Manny's goal is to sneak across the Rio Grande at night, to flee north into a new life.

After introducing each of these characters separately at the beginning of *The Crossing*, Gary Paulsen brings them together in a series of three chance meetings. In the first, Manny is passing through a Juarez alley when he comes upon Locke, drunk and throwing up. He tries to pick the soldier's wallet, but even in drunkenness Locke is alert, and he grasps the boy by the arm and begins to take him to the authorities. Meeting a police officer on the street, however, Locke has a change of heart and lets Manny go.

Locke and the boy meet a second time a few days later. Manny is begging food in the marketplace when he sees the tall American soldier enter a hotel nearby. The boy follows, and he manages to convince the already drunk sergeant to buy him breakfast. After eating, Manny accompanies Locke to a bullfight, and as the soldier awaits the coming slaughter of the bull, staring down at the animal, he softens and whispers, "All of this is [supposed] to mean something [but] it's for nothing. Only a game" (*Crossing*, 94). The soldier, who has faced death often, cannot bear to watch the senseless killing of the bull in the arena. Seeing it to be all too much like the senseless killing of his comrades in war, the soldier leaves the bullfight in a hurry.

A final meeting occurs when, a week later, Manny again runs into the officer. His life becoming more and more desperate, Manny decides to tell Locke "the truth" about his struggles to survive, and the boy begs the soldier to help him. Hearing this cry for help, Robert Locke is reminded of other such cries he has heard "in the green places when they had been hurt, hurt to death, and asked him for help leaning against the earth; with the dry spit in their voices and the short panting of their breath and there was nothing he could do for them then" (106). This time, however, Locke realizes that he can help, and "to his [own] complete amazement" (109), he promises Manny his assistance.

The Crossing is wholly different in tone from *Winterkill*, but each of the two books has a similar denouement. Just as Duda becomes vulnerable in reaching out to help another, so Sergeant Locke loses his soldierly armor as he begins to think of his future helping Manny. Walking through the streets of Juarez, the two come upon four men who had earlier tried to kidnap the child into slavery. As they come after Manny, Locke attacks and brings the men down, but in doing so he is cut by their knives. Dying on the pavement, Locke loses his soldierly fierceness and, to Manny, "the tall one's eyes became the same as the bull's eyes." Taking the wallet Locke has given him, Manny sets out to "run in the dark, run for the river and the crossing" (*Crossing*, 114).

Gary Paulsen at first expressed surprise when told of the similarities between Duda and Sergeant Locke, remarking, "They're two different characters" and observing that they were based on two different individuals he knew. Yet, after a brief reflection, the creator of both characters sees the parallel and quickly is able to explain why both mentor-warriors had to die. "There's no real future for either one of those guys in the sense that both had become corrupt. Anytime you have idealism, it becomes corrupt. It's inherent in idealism because whoever is idealistic will believe that it's worth anything, and when they start thinking that way, they will kill. They will do awful things for it. . . . [Not to kill them] would demean what they were."

On first consideration, Paulsen's reasoning appears curious, for it seems that just before their deaths both Duda and Locke are losing their hardness and corruption by becoming caring human beings. Paulsen seems to be saying, however, that broken warriors such as Locke and Duda never will lose all of their hardness, and that it "demeans them" to suggest that they are capable of such complete reversals.

What does this imply for the capacity of such warriors to nurture and guide? Certainly it does not mean that they lack such a capacity. Duda, after all, does have an extraordinarily positive effect upon his charge in *Winterkill*, and Locke does, consciously and willingly, help Manny. Actually, the deaths of the two men reveal more about the tragedy of their lot than about their capacity for love and concern. Ironically, as the men learn to give, their armor is stripped away. As they offer comfort and help, their own helplessness is assured. There are few more chilling portraits of the ravages of war.

Mr. Tucket and *The Car*

A second pair of books also expands Gary Paulsen's treatment of the adult mentor figure. In this case, interestingly enough, the pair includes the earliest of Paulsen's young adult novels, *Mr. Tucket* (published in 1968 and re-released in 1994), and one of his most recent, the 1994 work *The Car*. Examined together, the books suggest a possible evolution in Paulsen's thinking about the battered warrior, for in this case similar warriors are, in the end, viewed differently by the books' youthful protagonists.

It is 12 August 1845, and Francis Alphonse Tucket is traveling west in a wagon train across the Oregon Trail with his parents and sister. Francis has just celebrated his fourteenth birthday the day before, and his parents have given him his own rifle, a small but beautiful firearm they have carried with them all the way from St. Louis. Practice-shooting with his new gun, Francis forgets his father's warning and lags behind the train, and he comes to regret his carelessness when he is ambushed by a Cheyenne raiding party and taken captive.

The Cheyennes are led by Braid, a terrifying brave who gives Francis to one of his squaws and decides to take him along to a new encampment in the Black Hills. As Francis is about to abandon hope of ever escaping, a mountain man named Jason Grimes rides into the camp. Grimes is a ragged fellow with only one arm, and he is known well by the Cheyennes. (In fact, it is Braid who, in a fight, has caused the loss of his arm.)

Grimes recognizes Francis's predicament and, after helping him to escape, decides to take the boy along with him until they can rejoin the wagon train. Grimes, who takes to calling Francis "Mr. Tucket," comes to like the boy and begins to teach him about survival in the woods. He teaches the youth to shoot his gun, stalk antelope, and trap beaver discriminatingly so that the colony is not wiped out. Grimes also teaches Mr. Tucket about the ethos of the wilds. Francis cannot understand why Grimes is not vengeful toward Braid for the loss of his arm, and Grimes explains that the Cheyenne live by nature, that Braid took his arm in battle like a bear would have, and that there was no use in being angry at someone for following his nature.

After Braid's warriors raid the cabin of Grimes's friend Spot Johnnie and kill him and his family, however, Grimes sets out after the brave. He leaves Mr. Tucket with another wagon train before setting out, but the boy escapes and follows the mountain man, arriving just as Grimes, wounded again, manages to kill Braid. Mr. Tucket urges his mentor to leave, but Grimes, still filled with the exhilaration of battle, explains that he will first do what his adversary would have done, and he leans over Brave to scalp him.

In his revulsion, Francis Alphonse Tucket learns his final lesson from Grimes. He realizes that "Mr. Grimes was right. He *could* do what he was doing, simply because he was ruled by the same law that ruled Braid. He was of the prairie, the land, the mountains—and was, in a way, a kind of animal."[17] But just as quickly, the boy realizes that he himself is not such an animal. "There were different rules for different people. One set for Mr. Grimes, but Francis thought, as he reached his horse, there was a different set for him. He was *not* and did not want to be a 'mountain man'" (*Tucket*, 165). Without looking back, Francis Tucket mounts his horse and rides out headed west to Oregon, "to his family, to his kind of life—to his set of rules" (166).

Filled with savage Indians in war paint, struggling settlers on wagon trains, and action-filled but wholly unbelievable rescues, *Mr. Tucket* is a cliché-filled and predictable Western, certainly not one of Gary Paulsen's better works. The story generates at least occasional interest, however, through the character of Jason Grimes, a mountain man whose "animal" nature takes him several steps beyond the cliché. Grimes makes for an interesting mentor. Hardened by life in an unforgiving environment, he is still capable of concern for the young Francis Tucket, and he goes out of his way to befriend the boy. Still, when he reverts to his most-animal self and Francis prepares to leave, Grimes can say little more than, "It's been sort of fun having you around" (158). In the end, perhaps the greatest lesson Francis Tucket learns from Jason Grimes comes in leaving his hardened mentor behind.

Gary Paulsen's recent contemporary novel *The Car* is based on a similar mentor-student relationship, but it has a different resolution. Terry Anders, who is also 14, is an only child from Cleveland, Ohio, and like Francis Tucket is separated from his parents early in the book. In Terry's case, the separation comes after his battling, angry parents, "two people who just shouldn't have been together,"[18] both decide to leave home on the same day, each one not realizing that the other has left. For several days, Terry enjoys the quiet of being alone, but then he becomes fascinated with a "kit car" his father had left in the garage. The vehicle, a Blakely Bearcat, is a fully operational automobile, but it has to be put together, and so Terry, working day and night, assembles the machine (just as Paulsen himself assembled such a vehicle as an adult for a hobby—a photo of Paulsen with his Blakely appears on page 35). Terry comes to love the Bearcat (which he calls simply "the Cat"), and after finishing the assembly and taking the car for a test ride, he suddenly decides to pack the car, abandon the house, and leave his old life in Cleveland behind.

Terry Anders decides to head west to Oregon (curiously, the same territory Francis Tucket's family was headed for), where he hopes to locate an uncle, the only relative he has met. He plans to make the trip alone, but those plans are changed on the first day when he pulls off the road during a rainstorm. Huddled under a sheet of plastic in the small convertible automobile that has no top, Terry suddenly feels someone slip into the seat next to him, hears a man quote lines of Shakespeare about the rain, and comes face to face with Waylon Jackson.

Playing upon the opening lines of a noted poem by Lord Byron, Paulsen introduces Waylon to his readers in this way: "He walked in beauty. Wherever he went, no matter what was happening around him, to him, of him, he walked in beauty, in clouds of color, sprays of greens and blues and reds. He could see sunsets in a bus depot bathroom, hear Schubert in the roar of an engine, feel grace in a pile of mud" (*Car*, 39).

Waylon is in almost all ways a child of the 1960s. A Vietnam veteran with no roots and a vast, eclectic knowledge, Waylon for 20 years has been wandering across the country with nothing more than a backpack and his guitar. When asked by Terry what he does on his journeys, Waylon replies, "I am learning" (40).

Terry and Waylon team up, and youthful student and eccentric mentor strike out for Oregon together in the Bearcat. In many ways *The Car* proceeds for most of its length as a conventional journey saga—the story of lost souls traveling in search of their country and themselves. After teaming up with Waylon's Vietnam veteran buddy Wayne Holtz, the trio go off "trucking"—roaming the countryside directed only by their own curiosity. First they visit an ancient man named Samuel on the South Dakota prairie, who recites, as if he had been there, the battles between Sioux and soldiers occurring at that place a century before, and struggles for survival during the Great Depression, and accounts of draft riots in New York during the Civil War. Next they stop at a Mennonite commune to learn "how it is to live there" (129) and then travel to the town of Deadwood, where Wild Bill Hickock was murdered playing cards, and where Waylon wins a small fortune playing poker. Finally, they head for the Bighorn Mountains in Montana and Wyoming, the site of the massacre of General Custer's troops, where Terry learns how the slaughter there produced no winners, how Crazy Horse and his braves were later savaged in retaliation for that attack.

This is not a simple journey story, though, and Waylon and Wayne are not conventional guides. Through a chilling and effective series of war flashbacks early in the book, we learn what the Vietnam War had been like for Waylon and Wayne—how the two formed an assassination squad that snuck into enemy villages to "sanction" Communist supporters, and how Waylon had once had to kill a child. And we see the hard soldier emerge in the two veterans, and particularly in Waylon, several times during the journey. After a group of rowdy rednecks have harassed Terry and Waylon in the Cat, Waylon searches the men out and gains revenge, using martial arts moves (which happen so fast that Terry sees them only as "shrugs") to severely injure them. At the Mennonite commune Waylon "flips out" over their poor treatment of women and almost causes another confrontation.

Terry cannot understand this dark side of his traveling companion and asks Wayne about it. "Waylon's head is at a very, very hard place," Wayne explains. "Hard and cold and lonely" (85). When, after leaving the Custer memorial, the two veterans and Terry are again harassed by eight drunken rodeo cowboys in Buffalo, Wyoming, both Wayne and Waylon show the meanness of their military personas, and Terry is horrified at what he sees. Leaving town, the trio speeds up into the Bighorn Mountains, not as a means of fleeing, but (as the old soldiers revert to their military terminology) to "seek a more defensible terrain" (171). When Wayne and Waylon find a small rise, they stop and turn to face their attackers, and Terry realizes that the two are smiling, that they are looking forward to the fight. Waylon tries to explain their motivations to Terry, and he uses a rationale that sounds nearly identical to Jason Grimes's explanation in *Mr. Tucket* that he will scalp Braid because the mountain man is "an animal," because it is in his "nature" to do so. "We're doing this," Waylon explains, "because it is the way we are, have always been. It is our nature. Maybe because we want to do it." Also like Grimes, Waylon next disassociates his young companion from that world of meanness. "You don't have that problem," he says to Terry. "Now you leave" (*Car*, 176).

Terry Anders, like Frances Tucket, does leave after the bloody battle has taken place, but then in its last few pages, *The Car* totally turns the resolution of Paulsen's previous book upside down. Terry is back in his Cat, again heading west just like Francis did, and he thinks to himself, "I'll head west alone, see the world alone" (179). After only a few miles, however, Terry comes to realize that he is fooling himself, that he still needs, indeed wants, his ragged mentors with him. "Who would teach him to truck if he went alone?" (180), Paulsen writes, and Terry turns the car around and heads back to retrieve his friends.

One good reason that Terry's return to Wayne and Waylon works in a way that Frances Tucket's return to Jason Grimes never would have is that the two Vietnam veterans are drawn much more sympathetically than the mountain man. While Grimes simply "enjoys" having Frances along for the ride, Wayne and particularly Waylon go on the journey for the benefit of their young charge, because they are amazed at what he does not know about his country and what he needs to know. But all three battered warriors still carry the hardness of their fighting "nature," and Paulsen's different ending in the more recent book clearly represents a change in his thinking about the character of the mentor-soldier. Paulsen, it seems, has developed even more compassion for the plight of his battle-scarred veterans, and that compassion allows us to see them more as teachers and decent people, less as tragic animals who fight because it has become their nature. Terry Anders still has things to learn from Wayne and Waylon, and so he turns back to them. Perhaps Gary Paulsen is reminding us in this powerful book that we, too, still have things to learn from the broken, hardened soldiers among us.

Other Paulsen Mentors

While the 11 books analyzed above demonstrate the variety of adult mentors used in Gary Paulsen's fiction, there are a few others that provide one other view of this important character type in his work. Mr. Grimes may be the least redeemed and redeeming of Paulsen's mentor figures discussed thus far, but two other characters portray an even less sympathetic and helpful kind of teacher. Indeed, these characters—the carnival worker John in *Tiltawhirl John* and John Barron's great-grandfather in *The Haymeadow*—might be said to teach by counterexample, by showing, that is, what their young charges should not be and do.

In *Tiltawhirl John* the young narrator runs away from home and, after a series of other adventures, joins up with a traveling carnival where he meets Billy, Wanda, and John. John runs the tiltawhirl ride and has come to look sarcastically on the "suckers" who come to the circus. Giving them the "carny stare," John treats his customers with disdain. "They want you to ignore them," John explains. "It makes them feel like dirt, and that's what they want to feel when they come to the carnival. . . . I tell you, kid, people are puke—those people, earth people" (*T-John*, 79).

John's cynical division of all humans into "carnies" and "earth people" at first only amuses the book's protagonist as he comes to feel that he belongs among the carnival crowd. Ultimately, however, the young pupil comes to see the darkness and narrowness of his mentor's worldview, and at the end of the story he rejects John's philosophy, and John himself.

John Barron in *The Haymeadow* has grown up hearing the legends told about his tough great-grandfather, and he worships the man who claimed and settled thousands of acres of range land with only "a gun and two horses" (*Haymeadow*, 4). John makes the only four pictures taken of his ancestor into a poster for his room, and he puts his picture alongside it, remarking to himself how much he resembles the old man.

When John is sent to the haymeadow to tend the sheep, he tries to imagine what his tough great-grandfather would do each time a crisis arises. Always a hero to him, the old man becomes a kind of imagined mentor as well, teaching the young boy to be "tough" and to survive difficult situations. When his father comes to visit John in the haymeadow, however, the boy's view of his ancestor changes as father tells son the real story of the old man—of how he killed men brutally to seize the land and how, throughout his life, he scattered cruelty and meanness over his wife and family. As John begins to learn from his new mentor, the father who seemed always distant from him but who now shares time and stories with the boy, he is able to discard his great-grandfather as an unworthy role model and guide.

Both the narrator in *Tiltawhirl John* and John Barron in *The Haymeadow*, then, meet influential figures from whom they hope to learn. As they discover the flaws in these individuals, however, both boys learn a valuable lesson in casting them aside: that hero worship is dangerous, and that mentors with slanted and unhealthy views of the world are not the mentors to follow.

All in all, Gary Paulsen's adult mentors serve a vital function in his young adult novels. After acknowledging the problems of our age (environmental problems, nuclear war, bigotry) in a 1991 interview with Alice Evans Handy in *The Book Report*, Paulsen observed that our survival as a nation and people depends upon the next generation. Asked what could be done to ensure that survival, Paulsen responded, "We have to give kids all information as honestly as possible, as soon as possible, in the shortest possible time. I don't know the whole procedure for that, but I do know the that we're not doing it. I know that we're not giving them truth."[19]

Perhaps "giving them truth" describes best the role Gary Paulsen has bestowed upon his mentor figures. Whether loving relatives, concerned teachers, or battered warriors, all of Paulsen's adult mentors realize that the future lies in the hands of their young charges. With loving affirmations, careful instruction, and honest advice about how to live, Paulsen's mentors give his young characters, and his young readers, various lessons in "truth."

6. Laughing, Roaring, Singing: Paulsen's Other Voices

In the more than 100 books he has written, including several dozen for young adult readers, Gary Paulsen has experimented with a variety of approaches and dealt with a broad range of subjects. "I just hate to be limited," he has said, "and there's something really limiting about certain things. If you start a certain way, they [critics and readers] say you're supposed to be that way. Well, I don't know; you can move around a little bit. And so I've done that in several works."

Gary Paulsen's desire to "move around a little bit" has taken him beyond his intense focus on rite-of-passage and survival themes and his interest in the mentor figure into other topics and themes representative of his broad interests. But it is not diversity of topics that seems to capture the variety of his work; nor is it his range of themes. Instead, the closer one looks at Gary Paulsen and his collected work, the clearer it becomes that it is his willingness and desire to employ different voices that describes his eclecticism. Aside from the anxious and determined voice of the survivor, the questioning voice of the young person coming of age, and the soothing, helpful voice of the mentor, at least three other voices are audible in his works. One of these is a happy voice, the sound of a smirking giggle or full-bellied laugh. Another is a voice raised in anger, a roar or tight-throated growl. Finally, there is the voice of the singer, one who uses language to make music or to re-create the beauty of the other arts—dance, painting, and sculpture. Laughing, roaring, and singing are the sounds made by Gary Paulsen's other voices.

The Voice of Laughter: Paulsen's Humorous Novels

"I love writing humor," says Gary Paulsen. "It's fun to do, but it also is a really good way to set a stage or build a frame [for what you are writing about]. People become very receptive, and while they're receptive you can slide down in there."

In some of Paulsen's books humor is clearly being used to set a stage so that he can "slide down in there" to explore something that is not, in itself, funny. *The Island* is a good example. This somber and meditative book is filled with humor, particularly at the beginning. Wil Neuton's father holds "family conferences" with his wife and son that never get anywhere, hatches wild and impossible get-rich schemes (growing berries is his latest), and prides himself on being a home handyman (always insisting that Wil come along to "help.") The book's narrator reports on these repair efforts: "Three times in his life [Wil] had witnessed his father versus plumbing. It was never pretty, although he learned some interesting new words that his father had been saving for plumbing ever since he'd been in the army" (*Island*, 18). Humor is also created in *The Island* through the character of a craggy old town repairman, Emil Aucht, whose face is "like a live Halloween mask" (13) and who sprays tobacco juice out of his toothless mouth whenever he says his own last name, and through the bumbling therapist who tells Wil to call him "Chuck" when he introduces himself. (Wil, the narrator tells us, is tempted to respond, "What's up, Chuck?" but realizes how humorless the therapist is and decides against it [183].)

A similarly comical situation is used to introduce the artist Mick Strum in the book *The Monument*. Mick has rolled into town late at night in his rusty station wagon and, drunk, has somehow fallen asleep in the driver's seat—upside down. As the book's protagonist Rocky and her dog Python approach the car the next morning, they are greeted by a strange sight. "Jammed into the driver's-side window was the bottom of a man," reports Rocky, and when she comes closer and the bottom still does not move, she says to Python, "It's dead maybe; it's a dead bottom" (*Monument*, 50–51).

Mick eventually gets the driver's door open as Rocky approaches, but when he looks out, still propped upside down, he first sees the snarling Python, not Rocky. "Oh God, it's death, death coming for me," he squeals. "I've gone too far this time. I'm gone." As he turns his head, he looks up through his legs and sees Rocky for the first time. Smiling, he asks, "Tell me—are you with death?" (52).

Gary Paulsen is also not afraid to laugh at himself in his books. In *Woodsong* he creates a comical scene of a banty hen named Hawk who lives in the yard on their small Minnesota farm. After 14 abandoned grouse eggs that Paulsen finds in the woods are placed in Hawk's nest and they hatch, Hawk takes to protecting the new chicks by dive-bombing everyone who comes into the yard, and Paulsen offers readers several comical portraits of family members running for cover. In the same book, as he sets up a scene in which he is fishing in a canoe, Paulsen laughs at himself by explaining, "I was trying to catch a muskie so I could let it go" and then adds the parenthetical aside, "I do not understand why I was doing this either—I have never caught a muskie so I could let it go, though I have tried for several thousand casts, and have to a large degree stopped trying to catch a muskie so I can let it go" (59).

Even Paulsen's survival books contain humor. In *Hatchet* Brian Robeson at one point is butted repeatedly and almost killed by an angry moose. Later, when a tornado comes and destroys Brian's whole camp, he allows himself a moment for humor. "I hope the tornado hit the moose," he thinks to himself (158).

In addition to novels enriched by occasional humor, Gary Paulsen has written a few books that are, straight and away, just plain funny. In these books he is not so much using humor to set a stage or lighten an otherwise somber situation; rather, he seems simply to be enjoying the pleasure of funny situations. The only response to books like *The Boy Who Owned the School* and *Harris and Me* is sustained, hearty laughter.

The Boy Who Owned the School

Gary Paulsen confesses to being very shy when he was a teenager, and he reports that his son Jim was also shy as a teen. In a school production of *The Wizard of Oz* one year, Jim was given the job of hiding under the stage and running a machine that would propel smoke out onto the stage when the Wicked Witch of the West appeared. Unfortunately, Jim pumped the machine up so high that the relief valve let go. Gary Paulsen, who was in the audience, reports what happened next: "I heard this 'whoosh' under the stage, and then this one clear swear word. It rang through the audience, and we were all rolling on the floor. And the smoke came barreling out from under the stage."

His son's embarrassing experience becomes the climactic event in Gary Paulsen's novel *The Boy Who Owned the School*, a book he subtitles "A Comedy of Love." Jacob Friesten is a painfully shy teenager whose approach to getting through high school is to maintain complete invisibility. "If you get noticed," Jacob warns, "bad things happen,"[1] and when on occasion he is noticed, his prophecy invariably comes true. When a group of jocks stop him as he tries to sneak past their lockers, for example, they toss him around like a sack of potatoes and finally stuff him into a trash barrel outside the girls' restroom. On another occasion Jacob races into gym class late so that he will not be seen, but not watching where he is going, he runs straight into Maria Tresser, "the most beautiful, the most popular, the most everything girl in school" (*Boy*, 23), and the girl Jacob has a terrible crush on.

So Jacob works at being invisible. He times his entrances into the building each morning, perfects his downward "non-look" while teachers are asking questions in class, and studies the traffic flow in the halls so that he can move along them unnoticed. To counteract her son's shyness, Jacob's mother tries a form of positive reinforcement she has read about in a magazine, greeting him each morning with, "Good morning—and how is the boy who owns the school today?" (1).

One day Jacob's English teacher tells him after class that he is flunking because he does not participate, and she tries to help by assigning him the extra-credit project of operating the fog machine at the school's production of *The Wizard of Oz*. Jacob becomes even more panicked when he finds that Maria Tresser has the lead role, and despite his infatuation with her, he does whatever he can to avoid her during practices.

On the night of the play, Jacob becomes distracted and makes the same blunder that Paulsen's son did. As smoke pours out of the trap door in the stage floor, Maria stumbles through the opening into Jacob's arms. So shocked that he does not think, Jacob invites her for a date and is wholly stunned when she says yes. On the date Jacob tries hard to avoid his usual clumsiness, but he still knows that all the jocks who have seen him with Maria will jam him down into the trash container the next day, and he cannot help asking her why she has gone out with him. "Because you're a winner," Maria replies, and Jacob finally realizes that things are "perfect" (85).

Critics have praised this improbable and wholly likable book for its "sharp wit and incredible energy"[2] and for its ability to capture "the humor and painful injustice of early adolescence."[3] A reviewer in *Horn Book* calls it a "screamingly funny piece of writing,"[4] and indeed, it is Paulsen's humor that energizes the work. Jacob's mishaps are startlingly recognizable to anyone who has gone through or is going through adolescence, and so are the stereotyped characters (rowdy jocks, beautiful cheerleaders, stupid gym teachers) that fill the book. But Paulsen is determined to smile upon the whole difficult experience, to remind us that awkwardness can be as funny as it is painful. In making the shy Jacob "a winner," Paulsen justifies the laughter over his mishaps, for we know that we are ultimately laughing with Jacob, not at him.

Harris and Me

In the spring of 1950, Gary Paulsen and his parents were living in Laporte, Minnesota, having just moved back to their home state from Washington, D.C., where Gary's father had been finishing out his military career. Young Gary's life was anything but settled at that time. His parents' drinking had intensified, and he was spending increasing amounts of time living with relatives. As summer came, he was sent to live with another family of distant relatives: his mother's cousin, the man's wife, their 14-year-old daughter, and their 9-year-old son. *Harris and Me* is Gary Paulsen's loosely autobiographical account of that rollicking summer with his second cousin.

Paulsen remembers the summer of 1950 in this way: "I never saw Harris [the name given his second cousin in the book] wear anything but bib overalls with one of the shoulders unfastened. He never wore shoes, he never wore a shirt. I never saw him except in a full-blown run. And he turned me into a machine much like him, which is to say that we would get up early in the morning and have breakfast, and then we would get in trouble. And that's all we did all summer, we got in trouble, and Harris would think things up that would cause specifically me to get in trouble" ("GPR").

Harris and Me contains all the mischief and tomfoolery that one would expect when two young boys filled with imagination and nerve come together. Already on the first day, Harris coaxes the narrator to play war, and imagining the farm's pen full of pigs to be "dirty commie japs," they sneak up and then leap headlong onto the startled pigs, becoming covered with mud and pig manure as they are nearly trampled by the frightened animals. Later they try to play Tarzan by swinging on a rope from the granary roof, imagine themselves as Gene Autry as they leap out the barn loft door onto one of the huge workhorses, and rig up a motorized bicycle using the motor from the family washing machine. The catastrophes continue day after day.

One thing that makes *Harris and Me* so entertaining is that the boys' mischievous episodes are so imaginatively played out. Paulsen recalls that Harris's "one shining ability" was that "he believed everything was real" (*Harris*, 62). And so when he jumps on the pigs, he does so with passion because he truly sees them to be "dirty commie japs." When he leaps onto Bill the workhorse pretending to be Gene Autry charging off to "save" the rustlers (Harris always gets details mixed up and thinks that you "save" rustlers rather than "get" them), and he is bucked and kicked by the terrified horse, all he can say when his companion runs up to him is, "Did we save the rustlers?" (99).

Another reason for the delight of *Harris and Me* is Paulsen's pace in telling the story. The boys literally race from one adventure to another in the book, in the same way that most youngsters do, in fact, fly from activity to activity without pause as they are playing. The narrator's first day on Harris's farm is so packed with activity that by the time it is over and the tired boys flop into bed, 60 pages—more than one-third of the total number in the book—have already been turned.

A third and final way that Gary Paulsen creates humor in *Harris and Me* is by using an adult perspective to provide playful rationales for the mischief the boys get themselves into. Perhaps the most hilarious episode in the book tells of the narrator trying to think of a way to get revenge on Harris for embarrassing him in front of a girl. Harris's father has just installed an electric fence, and the narrator notices the shock Buzzer the cat gets when he brushes up against it. Suddenly, the young narrator becomes a student of electrical currents: "I had always been of a scientific nature, believed in the worth of experiments, and I wondered what would happen—watching Buzzer and the fence at war—if somebody actually peed on the wire. Specifically I wondered what would happen if *Harris* peed on the wire" (128).

After tricking and bribing Harris to attempt the stunt, the narrator "studies" the consequences: "The results were immediate, and everything I could have hoped for from a standpoint of scientific observation, not to mention revenge. In a massive galvanic reaction every muscle in Harris's body convulsively contracted, jerking like a giant spring had tightened inside him" (132).

Harris and Me is a highly entertaining collection of childhood adventures, full of energy, imagination, and mischief. It shows Gary Paulsen to be a first-rate writer of humorous prose.

The Voice of Rage: Paulsen's Angry Stories

Gary Paulsen is talking about what we have done to our environment, and he is angry.

> We have probably destroyed the planet. God, pigs don't crap in their bed, do you know that? They go in the corner of their nest and crap in the same place. Pigs! Imagine being dumber than pigs. . . .
> We're polluting the planet. We've put ourselves on the edge of a nuclear holocaust of terminal proportions. . . . We still use hair spray even though we're destroying the ozone level. We still kill whales. Why? Adults have made that happen—including me. We have been stupid. We have been lazy. We have done all the things we could to destroy ourselves. If there is any hope at all for the human race, it has to come from young people. Not from adults. We're too old. . . . We blew it. ("SFF," 12)

Remembering the respect with which Gary Paulsen treats the natural world in his outdoor survival books, it is easy to understand why his voice rises in anger when he considers the condition of our planet today. And it is not hard, either, to make a list of other issues that bring him to rage: the blind stupidity and utter devastation of war, the cruelty of racism, the injustice of gender and class discrimination. In Paulsen's treatment of all of these issues, one can hear him scowling at people's cruelty and carelessness and pleading for, even demanding, compassion and justice.

Sentries

Sentries is Gary Paulsen's most structurally complex young adult novel, and while it has not been one of his better sellers, it is clearly one of his personal favorites. The book is a montage of scenes and images that tell the stories of four teenagers who are living through experiences that will help them to come of age. Sue Oldhorn, 17, is a full-blooded Ojibway who lives in Minnesota, works in a bank, and becomes impatient and embarrassed when her grandfather delays dinner each evening to recite stories of their people's past. David Garcia is 14 and has just entered the United States illegally from Mexico to find work. After hitchhiking to Nebraska, David finds a job hoeing in the sugar beet fields. Laura Hayes lives with her parents on a large sheep ranch in Montana. A senior in high school, Laura loves working on the ranch, but her father thinks she should spend less time there and more time with her friends. Peter Shackleton has been out of high school for a year, and his rock group, Shackleton's Ice, is starting to receive attention and suddenly finds itself with its first big break: a chance to play a concert at the Red Rocks Festival in Colorado.

Each of these stories is told in four different vignettes, and most are resolved happily. Sue meets Alan, an Ojibway who asks her, "Are you whole?"[5] and through him she comes to appreciate her heritage. Laura helps her parents through several exhausting but fulfilling days of lambing and is able to convince her father that she works on the ranch not out of duty to the family but because she truly loves it. Peter goes in search of something new to play at the group's big concert and finds it in the wailing jazz sounds he remembers hearing once in a club in Kansas City. The performance of Shackleton's Ice at Red Rocks brings down the house. Only David's story does not end happily. Learning of the impossibility of making a living hoeing beets and of the unfair treatment of illegal immigrants on the beet farms, David feels anger well up in him and grimly holds on to it as a way of getting through life.

In reading *Sentries*, however, it is not just the success or failure of these four characters that one comes to care about, for the stories are also interspersed with other brief scenes that Paulsen calls "Battle Hymns." The first three of these tell the stories of veterans from, respectively, the Vietnam War, World War II, and the Korean War. All of the stories are horrifying; all portray soldiers who have been physically or emotionally destroyed by their war experiences. The fourth Battle Hymn, which concludes the book, is the shortest, and it takes us to a wholly different setting, a jungle in India where a Bengal tiger cares for her cubs, where we are shown the shocking suddenness of a nuclear holocaust.

In *Sentries* Gary Paulsen has taken some artistic risks, and the result has not always been successful with readers. Writing in the *ALAN Review*, Ronald Barron reports that students he worked with felt Paulsen was "teasing them with each part of the story" and became impatient with its fragmented narrative.[6] A reviewer in the *Bulletin of the Center for Children's Books* comes to the same conclusion, criticizing the book for its "rather gimmicky structure."[7]

Gary Paulsen stands by the book, though, and talks about it every chance he gets. "I was trying," he explains, "to get war to a level where young people could understand how bad it is. The battle hymns in there are absolutely true. They're not exaggerated, not fictionalized. All of those things happened. I went to soldiers' homes and nursing homes and talked to these guys."

To patient and attentive readers, *Sentries* does produce a real impact, and the book's power comes in part from the juxtaposition of scenes showing young people being young people (hoping, struggling, questioning), with images of war that are grotesque and unsettling. The disjointed structure of *Sentries*, it would seem, is part of the point of the book, for it shows war rudely breaking in on people's lives in the very way war does intrude on all sorts of people, and particularly on the young.

How is Gary Paulsen's anger heard here? Certainly not through hollering and shouting, for the book is, if anything, understated in tone and rarely raises its voice. But the anger is still audible. In having war intrude roughly on the stories of his young characters, and thus on his readers, Paulsen creates the effect of one hissing out a warning, spitting in a throat-tightened voice and at low volume the reminder that we cannot presume peace and order, that we must be watchful of those who bring us to the edge of conflict. That we must all be sentries.

Sisters/Hermanas

Gary Paulsen has admitted to "taking chances" in his recent fiction for young adults, and the slim book *Sisters/Hermanas* is evidence of that risk taking. In fact, Paulsen's agent Jennifer Flannery acknowledges being uneasy when, in delivering the manuscript to Paulsen's publisher, she had to tell him that it was only 60 pages long, that it was about a cheerleader and a teenage prostitute, and that Paulsen wanted the book printed and bound with English and Spanish language versions back-to-back.[8]

Sisters/Hermanas tells the parallel stories of two 14-year-old girls who live in the same large Texas city. One is Rosa, who has fled her home in Mexico City and has come north with the dream of one day becoming a fashion model. Rosa lives in a rented room in a tumbledown motel, the only place of her own she has ever had. While the girl is mostly illiterate, she can compute numbers and keeps a log of her earnings and expenses, which serves as a record of her progress toward her dream.

Rosa has brought almost nothing with her from Mexico except good memories of her mother (to whom she sends some money each week), a devout faith that brings her to set up a small shrine of Mary and the baby Jesus in her room and that motivates her to begin each day with prayer and attend Mass each Sunday, and a memory of poverty so extreme that she will do anything to avoid having to return to it.

And so Rosa sells herself. Each night she dresses in the provocative clothes she has bought with her earnings and goes out to stand on the street corners of the city. Some of the men are nice to her, but others are rough and hurt her. Still, she does what she has to do to avoid poverty and to move toward her dream.

Paulsen's second female protagonist has a dream also, but hers is the dream given her by her mother: "to marry well. To marry money. To have a wonderful, successful life with a fancy home and drive a Mercedes and have servants and travel all over the world—to the clean places, of course, not the dirty ones."[9] This girl, Traci, lives in the suburbs, is also 14, and seems to have a perfect life. Born and raised to believe that "nothing was ever bad, nothing was ever impossible, nothing was ever ugly, nothing was ever, truly, wrong" (*Sisters*, 21), Traci lives in that belief, except for odd, distracting moments when another view of life sneaks into her consciousness and she finds herself thinking, "Somewhere [life] isn't perfect" (22).

We meet Traci as she is ready to undertake the first great test of her youth, a test that, according to her mother, "counts more than anything you'll ever do in your life" in leading her toward her goal (42). Traci is on her way to high school cheerleading tryouts.

Paulsen leads us, in alternating chapters, through Rosa's preparation for another day of work and Traci's preparation for the tryouts. As Rosa prays and dresses in her short leather skirt and high-heeled boots, Traci carefully puts on her makeup and looks over the huge wardrobe in her closet. As Rosa reviews her ledger and counts her money, we learn that Traci's mother has paid a dance arranger $1600 to create an original cheer routine for her daughter.

Traci's tryouts are a great success, and her mother decides to celebrate by taking Traci to the mall to buy her a new outfit. Rosa, too, heads for the mall, but for a different reason. She has been seen by police officers while walking to work and, fearing that she will be arrested and deported, she ducks into the mall to hide. In a women's clothing store, as Traci looks over a rack of dresses, Rosa races in to avoid the security officers and hides among the dresses on the rack. Traci's reaction is startling. As her eyes meet Rosa's, she finds herself thinking, "We are the same" (64).

Traci's mother, of course, has a different reaction. She calls for the security guards and at the same time shouts to Traci, "Get away from her. Don't touch her" (65). As the security officer comes and takes Rosa away, Traci tries to tell her mother of her strange attraction to the girl, of how she thought the two were "the same." "No you aren't," her mother quickly replies. "She is what . . . she is what you might have been, could be, if you weren't like you are now" (66). And the mother leads her daughter's attention back to shopping.

While the figures in *Sisters/Hermanas* are stereotypical, the images are so jarring and the writing so terse that the book builds powerfully. Paulsen here is, between the lines and sometimes within them, raging—roaring in anger over two girls who are being used. Rosa's victimization comes at the hands of her johns (acknowledging recent history, Paulsen gets in a special jab here by making one of her regular customers a television evangelist) and at the hands of a society that forces some to seek survival in the basest of ways.

Traci, too, is a victim. Paulsen tells of a personal experience that shaped his creation of her character. "I was in a Texas gym one time, walking across the gym in a middle school, was going to do an appearance at the school, and there was a group of high school girls, seniors in high school, who were, mind you now, passing judgment on seventh grade girls, on whether or not they would be able to be good enough to be cheerleaders when they got to be seniors. And if they said 'no' it would kill these girls, it broke their hearts. And as I walked through they turned a girl down, and she ran from the gym sobbing. Her whole life was ruined. My God, she was twelve or thirteen. And her life was destroyed by these girls" ("GPR").

Traci is victimized by a peer system that honors such things as cheerleading beyond all bounds, and she is certainly victimized by a mother who seeks to live through her daughter's glory and who gives the girl a wholly skewed and unreal picture of life.

Gary Paulsen manages in *Sisters/Hermanas* to shout out angrily in two ways. When we realize how different Rosa and Traci are, how totally opposite are their ways of living, we hear the cry of injustice. And when we recognize their similarities, that they are both being raped of their young lives, we hear Paulsen's anger toward victimization.

Other Angry Moments

Sentries and *Sisters/Hermanas* both give us voices that are pitched throughout by impatience or rage, but it is possible in many of Paulsen's other works to also hear moments of his anger. Paulsen speaks out against cruel treatment of different racial and ethnic groups. In *Nightjohn* he makes readers squirm with the brutality of slavery, and even in the book's dedication he alludes to its cruelty: "This book is dedicated to the memory of Sally Hemings, who was owned, raised, and subsequently used by Thomas Jefferson without benefit of ever drawing a single free breath" (7). Paulsen unsettles his readers over past and current mistreatment of Native Americans through the portrait of Billy Honcho in *The Night the White Deer Died* and the execution by soldiers of Coyote Runs in *Canyons*. We are given a sense of how dehumanizing it is for Eskimo villagers to live in the "standard government houses" shown in *Dogsong* and of how hopeless life is for Manny Bustos and the other Mexican children who live in the streets of Juarez in *The Crossing*.

Paulsen strikes out angrily at economic slavery in the portraits of Mexican immigrant workers in *Tiltawhirl John*, and he allows his character Waylon Jackson in *The Car* to express his feelings about unfair treatment of women as Waylon explodes at the women's subjugation in a Mennonite colony.

Perhaps, though, Gary Paulsen saves his greatest anger for his portraits of war. Paulsen knows firsthand the horrors of war and soldiering. He saw his own childhood and the lives of his parents severely damaged by his father's military career and the dislocations of World War II, and he lost many army friends during the Vietnam War. Paulsen's continuing rage and sadness over war emerges again and again in his portraits of broken war veterans: hardened Duda and his friend, the town drunk Carl Sunstrum, in *Winterkill*, the disfigured Foxman in *The Foxman*, sweet and shattered Carl in *Dancing Carl*, and the hollowed out, "perfect" soldier Robert S. Locke in *The Crossing*. Paulsen's books also reveal startling facts in the history of war: that four times as many soldiers died from disease as from battle injuries during the Civil War (*The Monument*); that after the Custer massacre the dead bodies looked like white stones scattered across the hills (*The Car*); and that after Napoleon's defeat at the Battle of Waterloo women and children went about the battlefield with pliers pulling teeth from the fallen soldiers that could be used to make dentures for members of the aristocracy (*The Monument*). In all of these facts about war and portraits of people broken in battle, Gary Paulsen shouts out his rage at the human arrogance and stupidity that allows war to occur.

The Voice of Singing: Paulsen's Treatment of the Arts

Much of Gary Paulsen's public persona derives from his exploits in running the Iditarod dogsled race and from his fame for writing immensely popular outdoor adventure stories like *Hatchet* and *The River*. To be sure, Paulsen is an ardent outdoorsman, by his own admission more comfortable in the woods than in a city.

This image, though, certainly does not reveal the whole Gary Paulsen. Rugged outdoorsmen do not cry, and both Paulsen and his characters shed tears. Outdoor adventurers are not particularly moved by beauty, but Paulsen is as sensitive to beauty as many of his young protagonists are. And burly woodsmen are not thought to be great lovers of the arts, but Gary Paulsen is.

Gary Paulsen is knowledgeable about, and has experience with, many of the arts. He has studied sculpture and written the script for a ballet, he fills his studio walls with paintings (including, but not limited to, works by his artist wife Ruth), and he regularly listens to classical music while he writes. Even Paulsen's speeches and informal conversations are filled with artistic metaphors. ["I love writing," he says. "I love the dance of it" ("TV").]

What is true of the writer is also true of his writings, for in Paulsen's novels characters both young and old listen to music, watch and perform dance, and admire sculpture, painting, and great literature. Paulsen's love of art is reflected in his writing in another way as well, for in some books Paulsen seems interested in replicating the experience of art as well as just talking about it. In these works, Paulsen's language itself takes on the sound and structure of music, and in them it is possible to hear Gary Paulsen singing.

The Winter Room

The Winter Room is a story that seeks to capture the nature and quality of life on a northern Minnesota farm in, perhaps, the 1950s. Eleven-year-old Eldon and his brother Wayne live on the farm with their parents, their great-uncle David, and Nels, a friend of David's who is about the same age as the old man.

The book is divided into four sections, and in each Eldon narrates the story of farm life during a different season of the year. In early spring, when "everything is soft,"[10] the smells come out of the thawing earth and the farm comes to life. The windows are opened to bring fresh air into the stuffy farmhouse, father heads for town to buy supplies, and the boys return to familiar chores and games in the farmyard.

Summer is a time of hard work. Plowshares are sharpened, horses are harnessed, and the plowing and planting of fields is completed. During thrashing time neighboring families gather to share the work and to sit down together to immense home-cooked meals. On a rare free day there is time for swimming at a nearby lake.

Fall is the killing time, a time Eldon hates more than any other. Despite the necessity of slaughtering animals for meat, Eldon cannot stand the process of killing chickens and a steer. Most of all, he hates the squealing of the pigs as their throats are cut and the thick blood smell as they are butchered.

In winter the farm becomes covered with snow, and life is quiet. It is during winter, though, that the family gathers each night after dinner in the farmhouse's "winter room" to listen to Uncle David tell the winter stories: Norse legends and stories of life in the north woods, stories that tell of courage, beauty, strength, and humor.

Eldon and Wayne look at the winter stories differently. As Eldon explains, "I always thought of them as stories and didn't think they were real," but Wayne "believed them" (*Winter*, 84–85). One night Uncle David tells the story of a mighty woodcutter who could light a match by swinging an axe over it and who could swing two axes into a piece of cordwood so that the wood split cleanly and the axes met in the middle. When the boys' father interrupts the story to say to David, "But that was you" (91), Wayne feels betrayed. No one could do such things with an axe, he assumes, and so the story must be a lie. Besides, that David has told a story about himself means that he must be bragging.

Confronted with Wayne's accusations, Uncle David becomes silent and refuses, over the ensuing days, to tell any more winter stories. One day, however, while the boys are hiding in the barn, they see David come in, pick up two axes, and become "young again" as he summons his strength. He swings the axes into a piece of cordwood, splitting it so that the axes meet perfectly in the middle. That night, David tells the winter stories once more, and as Eldon reports, "Wayne listened and I listened and I knew we would listen for always" (103).

The Winter Room is a beautiful exploration into the nature of belief. For Wayne the stories had to withstand the test of "truth" to be believed; for Eldon they were "just stories" and did not require belief. Both boys discover through David's actions that one story is indeed very real, and as a result they choose to believe them all.

There is more to *The Winter Room* than just that tender, simple story of growing up, however. Gary Paulsen reports that he wrote the book as a symphony, with each season being a movement in the whole work. Indeed, when examined carefully, the book clearly comes to resemble a musical composition more than a novel. There is almost no narrative structure to the book, for example. The first 32 pages, the section on "Spring," tells almost no story at all and indeed relates almost no happenings of that season. Instead, it is a collection of portraits. We are told about the size, appearance, and location of the farm. (It sits "on the edge of a forest that reaches from our door in Minnesota all the way up to Hudson's Bay" [9], and "it has eighty-seven cleared acres" [10].) In addition we take a tour of the farmhouse, entering each room as we go, and we are shown the barn and the farmyard. Through all of this, very little happens. This is portraiture, the setting of a scene—not narrative.

Much the same thing fills the "Summer" and "Fall" segments, and even most of the "Winter" part. When the story of the winter room actually begins, we are already on page 70 of a 103-page book. The narrative only becomes sustained after we have come to experience and know the beauty of the farm, after we have heard its song.

Listening to *The Winter Room* as a symphony also gives purpose to the book's preface, a section Paulsen calls "Tuning." Interestingly, when *The Winter Room* was published, this introduction was criticized as being "overwritten and overly earnest"[11] and "offputting."[12] Today it has become probably the most well-known piece in all of Paulsen's writing—read aloud in classroom and at teachers' conventions and reprinted again and again in articles about Paulsen's work.

"Tuning" sets up a proposition about reading and books: "If books could be more, could show more, could own more . . ." (*Winter*, 1). It then completes the hypothesis by suggesting that if books could, indeed, "be more," then this book would be filled with smells (followed by intense sensory description of the farm smells) and sound (followed by sounds of a farm) and light (again followed by glowing and glinting and reflected light in and around the farm). The conclusion that a book cannot have any of these (actually disproved by the very pile of images included in the section) is used as a device for calling readers into the book, for it is readers who bring to books "sound and smell and light and all the rest that can't be in books. The book," concludes Paulsen, "needs you" (3).

There is, without doubt, more than a little gimmickry in this short preface, but it is artifice that fits Paulsen's view of the book as a symphony. Here Paulsen is tuning his instruments, inviting listeners in. Before the baton is raised and the actual music starts, both writer and reader (musician and audience) are made ready for the performance.

The Winter Room is music, and Paulsen is singing it (or playing it) for us. His gift to us is the gift of the artist—something not to study and critique, but to listen to, and look at, and enjoy.

Other Portraits, Other Songs: The Arts in Paulsen's Works

Of Gary Paulsen's works for young people, *The Winter Room* is perhaps his most successful attempt to re-create the music of the natural world. Paulsen achieves the same effect in his adult reminiscence about farm life, *Clabbered Dirt, Sweet Grass*, in which, for example, after introducing plowing as the "first great music of summer," he creates the flow of that melody with the long, repeating sentence fragment, "Plowing and watching the black dirt turn, the blue-black dirt so dark you can see into it turn and turn over and over like an earthen braid while the seagulls float over the blade of the plow in the hundreds, float on invisible air one foot, two feet above the turning black-beauty dirt, looking down for worms to grab and swallow without landing, to shoot up into the air while another gull swoops down for worms turning like gifts in the black rich earth."[13] In many of his other works for young adults, however, Paulsen also pays homage to the arts, sometimes by briefly trying to re-create artistic beauty, sometimes by acknowledging the impact of the arts on his characters.

In *The Car*, for example, protagonist Terry Anders quickly discovers how important literature is to his mentor and traveling companion Waylon Jackson as he sees Waylon reading all the time. Waylon reads Shakespeare, in particular, because "he's absolutely, without any doubt, completely and far away the best writer of the English language who has ever lived. . . . If you want to learn, you study winners—you study the best. And I want to learn" (*Car*, 124). John Borne in *Tracker* acknowledges the significance of literature in his life in several ways. As he hears the beauty of his grandmother's way of talking, he feels as though "she were just about to break into poetry" (*Tracker*, 15). As he comes upon a silent deer at the edge of the farm pasture, he feels such beauty that he writes a haiku to try to capture it:

> The doe stood
> in puffs of steam
> waiting.

> (*Tracker*, 26)

Music also appears in Paulsen's work, in particular as an expression of natural beauty and self-fulfillment. As Russel Suskit finishes his "dreamrun" to manhood in *Dogsong*, for example, he creates his own "dogsong" as an expression of his oneness with the dogs and as a celebration of the understanding he has come to. In *The Cookcamp* the grandmother sings soft Norwegian lullabies to her grandson, and the sounds blend melodiously with the chirping of the birds and even the bold sounds of trucks and caterpillars being operated by the road crew. In *A Christmas Sonata*, whose title again suggests a musical composition, the child protagonist listens at night to the adults talking quietly at the kitchen table, and their words sound to him "like a song" (*Christmas*, 55). He hears the music of bells as he runs to the door to view the "real" Santa Claus that has stopped outside the store.

Dance also expresses characters' feelings. In *Dancing Carl* Marsh and Willy come to understand, watching Carl's beautiful movements, that his dancing is an expression of "how he wants things to be, . . . how he wants his feelings to be" (*Dancing*, 92). And in *The Island*, as Wil Neuton studies a heron at the edge of the water, he tries to recapture its gracefulness in dancelike movements that imitate the curves and the sweeping motions of the bird as it walks and flies.

Wil Neuton also takes up drawing as a way of coming to know and understand what he finds on the island. After sketching a heron, a frog, and a remembered pose of his grandmother, he begins to experiment with watercolors, realizing the importance of color in his images. As Wil learns to represent the world around him visually, he also starts to see himself in artistic terms. Drifting quietly in his boat, the trees and water and birds around him still and beautiful, Wil remarks, "I am a painting" (*Island*, 32).

Without a doubt Rocky Turner's maturation in *The Monument* also coincides with her coming to understand the nature of artistic expression and appreciation. After Rocky receives lessons on line, form, and shading from sculptor Mick Strum and is told to draw what she sees over and over again, Mick also gives her a book about the painter Edgar Degas, and its effect on her is profound. Staring at one of Degas's dancers in the painting *The Dance Master*, Rocky feels the desire to know everything about the figure and then begins to cry when she realizes that the real dancer who had been painted must be dead, and that she will never know her as a result. Rocky is comforted by her stepmother, who casually gives her an important lesson about art at the same time. "There's still the painting, isn't there?" asks Emma. "You have that. You will always have the picture, won't you? So [the figures in the painting] can never be gone" (*Monument*, 112).

Gary Paulsen concludes *The Monument* with a postscript about the significance of art to the book, and the statement says much about his use of the arts throughout his novels. After acknowledging the importance to him of Katherine Anne Porter's statement, "Art is what we find when the ruins are cleared away," Paulsen explains, "I wanted to show art, show how it can shake and crumble thinking; how it can own and be owned, sweep through lives and change them—how the beauty of it, the singular, sensual, ripping, breath-stopping, wondrous, frightening beauty of it can grow from even that ultimate ruin of all ruins: the filth of war" (151).

Paulsen's reverence for the arts appears throughout his writings, both in his capturing of the artistic voice in the songlike cadences of some of his passages, and in his dramatization and explication of the significance of art in people's lives. As Clay Borne explains to his grandson in *Tracker* while pondering the boy's experience in seeing a beautiful doe and then writing a poem about it that even he cannot fully explicate, "The best joy and beauty are the kinds that are unplanned, and the same is true of painting or poetry. Don't chew at it too much. It's beautiful, and it makes you remember a beautiful part of your life and that's enough" (26).

7. The Other Writer: Paulsen's Books for Adults and Young Children

With more than two dozen young adult works to his credit and nearly three million copies of those books sold, it is tempting to think of Gary Paulsen as having been always and only a writer for teenagers, but he himself never anticipated early in his career that his success would come in that particular field. Paulsen recalls being "aware of young people" as an audience upon the publication of his first young adult novel, *Mr. Tucket*, but acknowledges that, at the time, "it somehow never occurred to me that I'd build up a reputation in that particular field."

Paulsen's writing career actually began with his work on adult men's magazines, and the first books that he sold were intended for an adult audience. As he became known as a young adult author, Paulsen continued to write occasionally for older readers, and lately he has returned to adults as an audience because, he explains, in writing solely for teenagers he found himself sometimes "hitting walls" both stylistically and in the subject matter available to him. Gary Paulsen has also, over the years, written on occasion for younger children, and he has found satisfaction (and some notable success) in coming back to that audience in recent years.

The result of these developments is that, today, Gary Paulsen moves among audiences in his writing perhaps more extensively than any other young adult author. A brief review of his publications for both adults and young children will reveal the other writer that Gary Paulsen has been and is—one whose extensive curiosities and diverse motives have taken him easily into a variety of publishing markets.

Paulsen's Books for Adults

Gary Paulsen's early nonfiction publications for adult readers are evidence that he was following closely the adage to "write about what you know." His experience as a soldier motivated him, for example, to gather interviews with returning Vietnam veterans into *The Special War*, a magazine-length examination of that war published in 1966. Two years later Paulsen drew on his experiences in aerospace and missile tracking to write his first book, *Some Birds Don't Fly*, a humorous exposé about early failures in our country's missile program that, he laughs, "was an awful book and probably sold 12 copies."

After Gary Paulsen moved first to Taos, New Mexico, and then to Colorado in the 1970s, he took to writing about the construction work at which he was making a living. First came the 1976 Prentice-Hall book *The Building a New, Buying an Old, Remodeling a Used, Comprehensive Home and Shelter How-To-Do-It Book*, a publication that is, indeed, as extensive in its review of home repair as its title promises and that, as a result, still can be found on the nonfiction shelves of many public libraries. Two other do-it-yourself construction books followed shortly thereafter: *Successful Home Repair* in 1978 and *Money-Saving Home Repair Guide* in 1981.

Gary Paulsen's experiences on many relatives' farms during his childhood and his occasional return to agricultural work as an adult has made the family farm a common setting for his young adult novels. Paulsen has also studied and paid homage to the American farm in his adult writings, first in a detailed and appealing book entitled *Farm: A History and Celebration of the American Farmer*, published by Prentice-Hall in 1977, and then in his recent, critically praised tribute to farm life, *Clabbered Dirt, Sweet Grass* (1992).

Farm is an unusual combination of scholarship and anecdote. In early chapters we learn of the impact of the Revolutionary War on farming in America (it set back farming 50 years, claims Paulsen), the evolution of oxen and workhorses as sources of power on the farm, and the development of planting and harvesting techniques that increased yields. In chapter 9, however, entitled "The Way We Were," Paulsen moves beyond scholarly exposition by using his personal knowledge of farm life and the stories told him by farmers to "capture and portray some of the beauty and vitality [of family farming] before it's completely gone."[1]

Paulsen's desire to "capture and portray" family farm life is even more evident in *Clabbered Dirt, Sweet Grass*, a work that Debra Schneider in a *Library Journal* review called "a quintessential farm story . . . that lets the reader dream of simpler, kinder times"[2] and *Publishers Weekly* praised as being "powerfully elegiac" in its impact.[3] *Clabbered Dirt, Sweet Grass*, a book Paulsen says he "loved writing," follows farm life through the four seasons in the same way his young adult work *The Winter Room* did. The work is nostalgic, but it is also powerfully evocative of a lifestyle that included exhausting labor and frightening uncertainties—portrayed movingly, for example, in the portrait of a farmer whose nephew comes upon him crying and throwing up in the barn as he looks out at a torrential rain that is washing out his spring planting (*Clabbered*, 23). Paulsen's precise detail (his ability, for example, to name and describe particular brands and pieces of farm equipment); his use of stylistic repetition (such as in this line about potato harvesting: "A day and then another day and by the third day crawling along picking, by the third day there has never been anything else but picking" [84]); and his wife Ruth Wright Paulsen's beautiful accompanying paintings of farm scenes all work together to create the sonorous melodies of life on a family farm. As Paulsen recalled in a National Public Radio interview with Noah Adams, "When these people farmed . . . , you couldn't live that way. You couldn't make a living really. It was impossible. And yet they did it. And they did it and they raised families and they had—they had joy. They had great joy in their lives."[4] *Clabbered Dirt, Sweet Grass* re-creates the "impossibilities" of family farm life, but also the "great joy" of it.

Gary Paulsen's personal experiences have also figured largely in some of his other recent nonfiction books for adults. In 1989 Paulsen published a series of vignettes called *The Madonna Stories* intended as a tribute to women for their "core toughness" and ability to persevere in the face of great difficulty ("SATA," 82). Many of the *Madonna* stories come from his own experience: a portrait of his mother as a protector who had "the face of the tiger"; another portrayal of the experiences with his grandmother recounted in *The Cookcamp*; and companion descriptions of Clara, the wife of a butcher, and Anna, a nurse, who both show tenderness in the smallest gestures: a graceful wrist movement or a small glance of concern. While the stories are uneven in quality and impact, the best of them do convey with some power the heroism of women confronting the world.

Gary Paulsen's 1993 work *Eastern Sun, Winter Moon* derives even more directly from his own experience. Called an "autobiographical odyssey," the book tells of Paulsen's own growing up, from living with his mother at age four in an apartment in Chicago during World War II to his horrendous journey to and life in the Philippines, where he and his mother joined his father after the war. *Eastern Sun, Winter Moon* is gripping reading. From Paulsen's account of his mother's drinking and unfaithfulness during the war to young Gary's memories of a shark attack on board a ship crossing the Pacific, his views of bombed-out Manila, and his sexual and emotional abuse in the Philippines, one wonders how Gary Paulsen came through his childhood psychologically and emotionally intact. Part of the book's impact comes from the vividness of Paulsen's recollections (triggered, he explains, from a box of photographs his sister uncovered after their parents died), and part comes from his skill in re-creating the naïve innocence of a young child being swept along in a violent, tumultuous adult world. Told that his father has been sent to Manila to help in the "rebuilding" of the Philippine government, young Gary imagines him at work on "some big government building—like the Chicago Museum where Mother had taken me once" (*Eastern Sun*, 19). Hearing adults around him refer to people as "Flips," "Japs," and "Huks," the young boy adopts their language automatically, having no sense of how inflammatory it is.

Eastern Sun, Winter Moon is both the autobiography of a resilient survivor and a portrait of lost childhood. In it Paulsen demonstrates his ability to create powerful effects for adult readers with the same sort of understated, unadorned prose that distinguishes his work for adolescents.

Finally, Gary Paulsen has taken his adult nonfiction writing into that part of his experience that has had the greatest impact on his adult life, the running of sled dogs. In his 1994 work *Winterdance: The Fine Madness of Running the Iditarod*, Paulsen gives his most complete account yet of the running of his first Iditarod dogsled race across Alaska in 1983. The basic outline of the race is already known to readers of Paulsen's *Woodsong* and to those who have heard or read any of the many interviews he has given about the experience. In *Winterdance*, however, he tells new anecdotes about his training and race that, if anything, create an even greater sense of the relentless and obsessive passion that racing dogs becomes to the mushers. As Paulsen tells, for example, of a prerace run in which he ignored warning signs and was almost blown to his death into a steep canyon in a terrible snowstorm, we understand his reaction afterward of feeling "scared," but we are wholly unprepared moments later for his admission of what has actually scared him: "I thought that any sane man who was in his forties and had a good career going would quit now, would leave the dogs, and end it now and go back to the world and sanity and I knew what scared me wasn't the canyon and wasn't the hook hanging by one prong but the knowledge, the absolute fundamental knowledge that I could not stop, would not stop, would never be able to stop running dogs of my own free will" (*Winterdance*, 18–19).

Over his writing career Gary Paulsen has also dabbled in almost all of the well-known genres of popular adult fiction. He has written science fiction (in, for example, the 1977 book *Meteorite Track 291*) and well-received Westerns in the five-book

Murphy series about Al Murphy, the hardened and grimly determined sheriff of the small mining town of Cincherville, Colorado,
and the two-book Dirk series (published under the pseudonym
Paul Garrisen). Paulsen has also shown his ability to write suspense stories in nearly a dozen mystery-thriller novels written
over the last 20 years. The most recent of those, two books he
wrote for Donald Fine Publishers in 1989 and 1990, were widely
praised for their well-constructed plots and furious action.
Kirkus Reviews, for example, notes about the first of the books,
Night Rituals, that its plot elements are "handled with expert
care and rotated at such a rapid pace that the final result is satis-
fyingly gripping entertainment."[5] *Kill Fee*, the second, is
described in *Publishers Weekly* as "rich in detail, swift in plot,
and impossible to put down."[6] Clearly, Paulsen's ability to tell a
good story translates well even into the formulaic conventions of
mass-market fiction.

Paulsen's Books for Young Children

Gary Paulsen's struggles to make a living at writing in the 1970s
led him not only into various attempts at adult fiction and nonfiction, but also into writing nonfiction books for children. One
early project was a series of humorous sports books entitled
Sports on the Light Side done for Raintree Publishers. The books
in the series are distinguished by their long and whimsical titles
(for example, *Dribbling, Shooting, and Scoring Sometimes* and
*Downhill, Hotdogging, and Cross-Country—If the Snow Isn't
Sticky*) and their tongue-in-cheek view of the sporting world (not
surprising given Paulsen's severe reservations about whether
children should even participate in organized sports). All in all,
the works are uneven in quality, partly because readers remain
unsure about whether the books are designed to inform them
about sports or just to entertain them. One title in the series,
however, an overview of the sport of hot air ballooning entitled
Full of Hot Air, has remained popular and was reprinted by
Delacorte in 1993.

Paulsen is more effective in writing about activities he knows well and cares about. In the 1981 book *Sailing: From Jibs to Jibing*, for example, Paulsen again undertakes the task of informing young readers about a recreational activity, but this time it is one that has been an important pastime for Paulsen himself. As a result, while the tone is still light here, we hear in this book more of the voice of Paulsen the teacher and guide, patiently explaining sailing equipment and techniques and cautioning his young readers to practice safe boating procedures.

Gary Paulsen also tried his hand at writing biography in the 1976 work *Martin Luther King: The Man Who Climbed the Mountain*, co-authored with Dan Theis. The book focuses on King's public campaigns for racial desegregation rather than on his private life, and it is interesting, among other reasons, for its manipulation of chronology for dramatic effect. The book opens, for example, with a scene of King at the Lorraine Motel in Memphis just moments before he is shot, then flashes back through King's life and work, then leads back to Memphis with an explanation of what brought King there, making the climactic assassination scene particularly meaningful and tragic. In a *School Library Journal* review, John F. Caviston particularly praised the book's "substantive" treatment of King's guiding principles and its discussion not only of King's successes, but also of his failed attempts at desegregation.[7]

In recent years Gary Paulsen has turned his attention again to the young reader, this time not so much to sustain an income as to accomplish a purpose about which he feels strongly. Paulsen has expressed worry about the poor reading habits of many children and, particularly, about the effects of television on them. Out of that concern Paulsen began, in 1992, a series of short works called the Culpepper Adventure series whose purpose was "to steal them away from television" ("ABS") with fast-paced, easy-to-read stories filled with funny characters and outrageous adventures.

Like a television sitcom, the Culpepper books all make use of the same main characters, Duncan ("Dunc") Culpepper and his "best friend for life" Amos Binder, and each episode takes these friends on a different crazy escapade. Dunc is the bold, inquisitive one, who almost always initiates the pair's actions. Amos is his bumbling, comical pal, a boy who has doubts about adventure but who keeps getting enticed into Dunc's exploits by promise and trickery (the most common promise being that if he goes along he will become famous and the true love of his life, classmate Melissa Hansen—who "doesn't even know he exists"—will finally notice him).

The Culpeppers are sometimes boy-detective crime stories (with Dunc and Amos as younger and funnier versions of the Hardy Boys) and sometimes adventure tales. In *Dunc's Undercover Christmas*, for example, the boys uncover a crime ring of shoplifting Santas, and in *Dunc Breaks the Record* they become trapped in the wilderness (where Paulsen adds some extra fun by having Amos try unsuccessfully to use knowledge gained from reading a survival book called *Hatchet*). Sometimes, too, Paulsen takes the boys on supernatural escapades, as in *Culpepper's Cannon*, where Dunc and Amos travel through time and witness the Civil War sea battle between the *Monitor* and the *Merrimac*, or in *Dunc's Halloween*, in which Amos is bitten by a werewolf and starts to behave like a "werepuppy" by scratching himself and chasing trucks. Veracity has no bearing on the adventures, only action and comedy. Paulsen justifies that variety by again testifying to the purpose of the series—to grab young readers.

The series certainly has been successful in doing that. "They're going like popcorn," Paulsen laughs, noting that close to 500,000 Culpepper books were sold in the series' first year and remarking, with clear satisfaction, that he has even heard stories of young boys buying up copies and scalping them to friends. Paulsen himself enjoys the books so much that he plans to continue writing six more per year for the foreseeable future. "God, I have fun with those kids [the books' main characters Duncan Culpepper and Amos Binder]," he remarks. "I probably shouldn't, I mean it isn't decent to be having that much fun. I just die. I'll be laughing out loud in here [his office] while I work."

The success of the Culpepper Adventure books also led Gary Paulsen to undertake in 1994 a second series for young readers called Gary Paulsen's World of Adventure. Each of these action-adventure stories features a different set of male and/or female protagonists, and each involves some type of adventure of interest to preteens. In the first book in the series, for example, entitled *The Legend of Red Horse Canyon*, Will "Little Bear" Tucker and his friend Sarah try to find their way out of an intricate cave system in the Sacramento Mountains after becoming lost in the caves.

Finally, Gary Paulsen and his wife Ruth Wright Paulsen have collaborated on a picture book for very young readers and pre-readers. *Dogteam*, published in 1993, tells of a musher taking his dog team on a night run through deep woods and across a lake (based on Paulsen's run across Clear Water Lake in Minnesota described in *Woodsong* and elsewhere). The run is quietly beautiful, and both Gary Paulsen's text and Ruth Paulsen's illustrations capture that almost mystic beauty by focusing on the gracefulness in the dogs' movements and the wonder in their eyes. A second picture book collaboration between husband and wife, entitled *The Tortilla Factory/La Tortilleria*, is scheduled for publication in 1995.

Repetition in Paulsen's Writing

An obvious question to ask about any prolific author—especially one like Gary Paulsen who writes for such a variety of different markets—is how he or she is able to keep coming up with new ideas for new books. In the case of Gary Paulsen, part of the answer is revealed by recognizing his active imagination and obsessive work habits, but part also comes from understanding that, often, he does not invent new material. In other words, Paulsen sometimes writes new books that are based on stories he has told before.

This repetition is apparent to anyone reading any number of Paulsen's books. The same winter stories that are central to *The*

Winter Room, for example, appear also in *The Foxman, Popcorn Days and Buttermilk Nights*, and *Clabbered Dirt, Sweet Grass*. An episode about two boys playing cowboy by jumping out of a hayloft onto the broad back of a workhorse appears in three books: *Harris and Me, The Winter Room*, and *Clabbered Dirt, Sweet Grass*. A young boy's summer with his grandmother in a cookcamp in the northern woods is related both in *The Cookcamp* and in the story "The Cook Camp" in *The Madonna Stories*, and the backbreaking labor of hoeing sugar beets appears both in *Tiltawhirl John* and in David Garcia's story in *Sentries*.

What is the significance of this repetition? Is it evidence that Paulsen is, in fact, running out of ideas—that he is overly dependent on personal experience in his writing and thus must recycle the same vignettes through book after book? Not necessarily. In fact, there are two more likely explanations.

Certainly some of Gary Paulsen's reuse of events is due to his versatility in writing for various audiences. Assuming a different readership for each book, Paulsen sees no overlap in telling each of those types of readers the same story. And so, for example, life on a family farm during different seasons of the year is portrayed in the adult book *Clabbered Dirt, Sweet Grass* and the young adult work *The Winter Room*. Paulsen's experiences running dogs are told to adults in *Winterdance*, to adolescents in *Woodsong*, and to children in the picture book *Dogteam*. (In fact, Paulsen, who originally thought *Woodsong* should have been cross-marketed for both adolescents and adults, later found himself pleased that it was not because then he felt free to retell the story of his Iditarod experience "in another way" in *Winterdance*.)

Not all of Paulsen's recycling of events and details can be explained by audience differences, though. Even among works for readers of the same age there is noticeable repetition. Perhaps the other explanation for this reuse lies in Paulsen's view of literature as art. While he explains that "mining my life is what I do [in my works]," and that "I don't make things up much," Gary Paulsen has always felt free to use those life experiences to achieve a variety of artistic effects. For example, when Paulsen tells of the experience of "playing cowboy" by jumping onto a workhorse's back in *Harris and Me*, the effect is hilariously slapstick, befitting Harris's frenetic, derring-do personality. When the same scene appears in *The Winter Room*, it is also funny, but more quietly so, more in tune with the sweetness of that book's tone and of its main characters Eldon and Wayne. Same event, different effect.

Paulsen has often referred to writers as artists, making the point that a writer does not only tell what is or might be, but also controls the effect of that telling, as an artist controls mood, line, and color. Paulsen in his own writing, then, may certainly be experimenting with mood and effect as he retells stories. To him the beauty and awe of running the Iditarod conveyed in *Woodsong* is, in a sense, a different story from his account of a musher's relentless obsession with running the race in *Winterdance*.

Although Gary Paulsen himself has never made this connection, it is interesting that some of his personal preferences for artists and composers also show the same predilection for repetition. A lover of classical music, Paulsen acknowledges listening often to Beethoven, the composer who experimented with some of the themes and melodies of his great Ninth Symphony for almost 30 years (using, for example, an early Choral Fantasy as the basis for the Ninth's famous last movement) before gathering them all together in that work. Paulsen also has expressed a particular appreciation for the American artist Andrew Wyeth's Helga pictures, a collection of 240 drawings and paintings completed over 15 years, all using the same individual (Wyeth's neighbor and friend Helga Testorf) as its subject. Are there repetitions in Beethoven's compositions or Wyeth's paintings? Certainly, yes. Redundancies? No. And without doubt, Paulsen also sees no redundancy in his reuse of events and vignettes, for always it is the artistic purpose of the telling that shapes the vignette and makes it different from other tellings.

8. The Now and Future Gary Paulsen: Today's Writing and Tomorrow's Plans

Gary Paulsen Today

The pace of Gary Paulsen's writing in the 1990s has been breathtaking. From 1990 to 1993, for example, 11 new young adult books by Paulsen were published, along with 2 major adult works, 16 Culpepper Adventure books, and 1 picture book. Furthermore, his contractual commitments and personal writing schedule suggest that this pace will continue at least to the end of the decade.

Why? What does Gary Paulsen have left to prove, and why is he racing toward those goals at such a breakneck speed? Shortly after having heart problems several years ago, Paulsen claimed that he was picking up his writing pace because he still had lots of writing to do and was unsure how much time he had left. But that answer does not hold up. Paulsen today is in good health and has had no serious reoccurrence of heart difficulties. Nor is he driven by a desire for money. True, Gary Paulsen lived in poverty for much of his writing career, but in recent years his books have made him a wealthy man. "Besides," says Paulsen convincingly, "the money means absolutely nothing to me. I give it all to Ruth." Why, then? The only answer left that seems to make any sense at all is: for the pure fun of it, for the exhilaration that the writing brings. Gary Paulsen has always professed a love for the challenge of a task, for the doing of it. For him that was what running dogs was all about. In a 1992 interview with Noah Adams on National Public Radio, Paulsen tried to explain the passion he felt for being on a dogsled. After describing the all-consuming sense of beauty he experienced for a few minutes on one of his early runs in northern Minnesota, he explained, "I realized I would run a million miles if I could get ten minutes of that again" ("NPR").

When Paulsen could no longer run dogs, he was forced to seek beauty elsewhere, and that search seems to have driven him even more passionately into his writing. "I absolutely love to write," says Paulsen. "When a story works, the hair goes up on my neck" ("GPR"). Significantly, Paulsen rarely reads his finished books, and in discussing them his comments go almost automatically to the experience of writing them rather than to any assessment of their impact or worth for a reader. When asked about his favorites among his many books, for example, Paulsen says, "I kind of miss writing *Dogsong* sometimes. I had a good time with that, and *Clabbered Dirt, Sweet Grass* I loved. I just loved it. But there's always the next one too."

And so, always searching for the experience of "the next one," always trying to find the next 10 minutes of beauty, Paulsen writes. Often for up to 18 hours a day, seven days a week, Paulsen writes. When he is at home, Gary Paulsen typically rises at 5:30 A.M., meditates for a half hour, and then begins writing. He writes until noon, takes a short lunch break, takes care of a bit of correspondence, and then writes again until dinner. After another brief meal, Paulsen will either go back to writing or spend the evening researching and mapping out future books. It is typical, he says, for him to fall asleep around midnight with a book in his hands.

Even when his schedule is disrupted by travel and personal appearances, Gary Paulsen crowds as much writing into his days as he can. Wherever he goes, he brings along his laptop computer and writing tablets. On airplanes and in hotel rooms, he writes. Even sitting in a hotel lobby for a few minutes between appointments, Paulsen will pick up a tablet and write a page or two of a Culpepper Adventure novel. In the summer of 1993, Paulsen and a friend took a two-week motorcycle trip from his home in New Mexico to Fairbanks, Alaska, and back. Every day, when he was not riding, he wrote. And continually during his 1995 trans-Pacific sailing voyage, Paulsen would go below deck to sit in front of his laptop computer and write.

Gary Paulsen's obsessive work habits derive from his experiences training for and running the Iditarod, when he would often be on a sled for 18 hours a day. "The Iditarod makes people not normal," Paulsen explains. "It permanently affects the way you see things for the rest of your life and the way you do them. So that I don't just write; I write 18 hours a day. It's so strange because I don't recognize obstacles. That comes from the Iditarod too. I don't see something as a problem. I just go through it, and if something happens during the day that would keep me from writing, I just, well, I just won't do it. And I miss appointments. I just don't pay attention to the silly parts of life."

Gary Paulsen's writing room at home reflects this professional, no-nonsense approach to his craft. The room, actually a converted bedroom, is comfortably cluttered by piles of notes and correspondence, and there is little attention given to decoration, except for some paintings done by his wife and by a friend on the walls. A computer with large-screen monitor dominates his desk, and nearby is a telephone fitted with a headset so that he can rewrite or take notes while he is talking to editors and others. Dogs wander in and out while he works.

An essential piece of equipment in the room is Paulsen's compact disc player, on which classical music is playing almost continuously while he works. (Paulsen's favorite composers are Beethoven and Mozart, and he also listens to Mahler and Mendelssohn; his daily choice depends on "the kind of writing I am doing.") Through a window near his desk, Paulsen has a direct view of Sierra Blanca, a 12,000-foot peak that is about 20 miles north of his home. "It's stunning," says Paulsen, "and it changes its clothes every day—you know, changes the way it looks. It's hard to paint anything that beautiful."

While Paulsen may be researching several works simultaneous-
ly, he seldom does writing on more than one book at a time, and
he claims to have little problem in completing one project and
starting right up on the next. This is true even if the transition
includes changing from one audience to another—for example,
from writing an adult work to one for young adults. In fact, he
claims not to be preoccupied with audience at all, letting his
sense of the story and his concern for the book's purpose and
tone guide the writing.

Paulsen writes efficiently—the product, he says, of early training
in magazine writing where, "if I don't get it done, I don't have a
car payment." Although he often has a "mental outline" of where
he wants a book to go, he seldom takes the time to map it out
extensively on paper. Since learning to write at the computer using
word processing software several years ago, Paulsen has come to
enjoy the process of rewriting, feeling the freedom now to experiment with various versions of a passage to test their effectiveness.

Gary Paulsen has also come to appreciate the contributions of a
good editor. Richard Jackson, Paulsen's friend and former editor
at Orchard Books, was especially effective at helping him with his
work. "Someone like Dick," Paulsen notes, "gets inside your head
and enhances what you're trying to do." Paulsen's current editors,
Karen Groves at Harcourt Brace and Wendy Lamb at Bantam
Doubleday Dell, also have made useful contributions to his work.

Paulsen, however, does recall times earlier in his career when
editors were not always so helpful. For almost 20 years of writing
without having any clout ("when I was Gary Who? and they
weren't doing my biography"), Paulsen would spar with editors
again and again about what should go into his works. In those
battles he perfected a comical method of dealing with intransigent
editors—something he called "rabbit gardening." "When you garden and rabbits are bothering you," Paulsen explains, "you build
your regular garden here, and then over here you put in a little
rabbit garden with what they like. You put in peas and lettuce and
stuff that the rabbits really like, and you let them eat it. In some
of my early books, I'd put rabbit gardens in—just glaring mistakes
that editors could find. And quite often I was caught, and they'd

say, 'What the hell is this?'" ("GPR"). By planting "rabbit gardens," Gary Paulsen kept his editors busy and distracted them from other things he was trying to do in his books.

Paulsen's Future Plans

Gary Paulsen seems unsure of how to answer a question about his future plans, except to say, "I plan to keep writing. It's not about money and not about awards. I just want to write." Although he plans to keep publishing works for all audiences, he expects that much of his writing will continue to be addressed to young adults, and although he will still write nonfiction, most of his future books will be novels.

Specifically, Paulsen has nearly completed work on several young adult works due out in 1995. One, a novel entitled *The Tent*, is about a father and son who spend a summer "scamming" believers as bogus revival preachers—until the message of their fake sermons surprisingly starts to get through to them. Another will be entitled *The Rifle*, and in it Paulsen will risk using a rifle as his "main character" as he traces the ownership of the rifle from pre–Revolutionary War days up to the present time, all the while seeking to challenge the contemporary political adage "Guns don't kill people, people kill people." Finally, Paulsen has begun mapping out a novel (working title, *The Ride*) about a girl who handles racehorses and travels across the country from track to track with them.

Gary Paulsen also has several sequels to current works planned or under way. *Call Me Francis Tucket*, due out in 1995, picks up the story of his young adult western *Mr. Tucket* as young Francis heads West in search of his parents, and a third Tucket western is also being sketched out. Fans of Paulsen's most famous character, Brian Robeson, will be delighted to know that another book is being planned to follow *Hatchet* and *The River*. Tentatively entitled *Brian's Winter*, the book will be an "alternate sequel" to *Hatchet* that will answer the question, "What would have happened to Brian if he *hadn't* been rescued before winter came to the Canadian wilderness?" "I know an awful lot about winter survival," Paulsen observes, "and I think it would be interesting to see how Brian handles that challenge."

A third illustrated book done in partnership with Paulsen's artist wife, Ruth Wright Paulsen, is also in the works. Explaining that "I'm not quite done with the dogs yet," Paulsen is writing *Puppies, Dogs, and Blue Northers* as a nonfiction tribute to his beloved lead dog, Cookie. It will tell of the birth and training of Cookie's last litter of puppies, of Cookie's own retirement from dogsled racing, and of her death.

For adults Gary Paulsen intends to release another book in his Murphy western series, *Murphy's Ambush*, in 1995. He also plans to extend the autobiographical account of his life begun in *Eastern Sun, Winter Moon*, probably with two more books, the first of which will describe his teenage years and will, he says grimly, make the experiences described in *Eastern Sun, Winter Moon* "look like kind of a cakewalk" ("GPR"). And for young readers, Paulsen intends to continue the Culpepper Adventure series and the Gary Paulsen World of Advenure collection, publishing six of each annually for the foreseeable future.

No matter where his writing takes him, Gary Paulsen is certain to remain devoted to it, even obsessed by it. Almost 15 years ago, Paulsen described the motivations for his writing in this way: "I have two reasons for writing. I want my 67.9 years on this ball of earth to mean something. Writing furnishes me a way to make that happen. Secondly, I have not done anything else in my life that gives me the personal satisfaction that writing does. It pleases me to write—in the very literal sense of the word. When I have done well with it, and 'cooked' for a day so that it felt good when I put it down, . . . I go to sleep with an immense feeling of personal satisfaction."[1]

Knowing Paulsen's love of writing, and the immense energy he brings to his efforts, there is no doubt that young adults and others who read and admire Gary Paulsen's works will have more, much more, to read and admire in years to come.

Notes and References

Preface

1. All otherwise uncredited quotes from Gary Paulsen are from telephone and personal interviews conducted by the author on 13 September and 19 November 1993, and 7 March 1994.

1. Beginnings: The Young Life of Gary Paulsen

1. Gary Paulsen, *Tiltawhirl John* (Nashville, Tenn.: Thomas Nelson, 1977), 9; hereafter cited in the text as *T-John*.

2. Gary Paulsen, "Remarks at Harcourt Brace Gary Paulsen Reception," National Council of Teachers of English National Convention, Pittsburgh, 20 November 1993; hereafter cited in the text as "GPR."

3. Gary Paulsen, "ALAN Breakfast Speech," National Council of Teachers of English National Convention, Seattle, November 1991; hereafter cited in the text as "ABS."

4. Gary Paulsen, *The Madonna Stories* (New York: Harcourt Brace Jovanovich, 1989), 69; hereafter cited in the text as *Madonna*.

5. Gary Paulsen, *A Christmas Sonata* (New York: Delacorte, 1992), 64–65; hereafter cited in the text as *Christmas*.

6. Gary Paulsen, *Eastern Sun, Winter Moon* (New York: Harcourt Brace Jovanovich, 1993), 5; hereafter cited in the text as *Eastern Sun*.

7. *Trumpet Video Visits Gary Paulsen*. Holmes, Pa.: Trumpet Club, Inc. Videorecording; hereafter cited in the text as "TV."

8. Gary Paulsen, *Harris and Me* (New York: Harcourt Brace Jovanovich, 1993), 1; hereafter cited in the text as *Harris*.

9. Anne Commier, ed., "Gary Paulsen," *Something About the Author*, vol. 54 (Detroit: Gale Research Co., 1989), 87; hereafter cited in the text as *SATA*.

10. Alice Evans Handy, "An Interview with Gary Paulsen," *Book Report*, May/June 1991, 28–31.

2. *Lessons: Becoming a Writer*

1. Agnes Garrett and Helga P. McCue, eds., "Gary Paulsen," *Authors and Artists for Young Adults*, vol. 2 (Detroit: Gale Research, Inc., 1989), 168; hereafter cited in the text as *AAYA*.

2. Allen Raymond, "Gary Paulsen: Artist-With-Words," *Teaching PreK–8*, August/September 1992, 54.

3. Kay Miller, "Suddenly Fame and Fortune," *Minneapolis Star-Tribune Sunday Magazine*, 10 July 1988; hereafter cited in the text as "SFF."

4. Betsy Hearne, review of *Real Animals: The Grass Eaters* and *Real Animals: The Small Ones*, *Booklist*, 1 October 1976, 255.

5. Rich Davis, "North to Alaska," *Evansville Courier*, 8 March 1992; hereafter cited in the text as "NA."

6. Gary Paulsen, *Woodsong* (New York: Bradbury/Macmillan, 1990), 25; hereafter cited in the text.

7. Dorcas Hand, review of *Dancing Carl*, *Horn Book*, August 1983, 447.

8. Review of *Tracker*, *Bulletin of the Center for Children's Books*, June 1984, 172.

9. Gary Paulsen, *Winterdance: The Fine Madness of Running the Iditarod* (New York: Harcourt Brace Jovanovich, 1994), 255; hereafter cited in the text as *Winterdance*.

10. Review of *Clabbered Dirt, Sweet Grass*, *Publishers Weekly*, 29 June 1992, 48.

3. *Songs of the Earth: Paulsen's Survival Stories*

1. Review of *Woodsong*, *Booklist*, 15 March 1991, 1472.

2. Review of *Woodsong*, *Publishers Weekly*, 27 July 1990, 234–35.

3. Gary Paulsen, *Hatchet* (New York: Bradbury Press, 1987), 51; hereafter cited in the text.

4. Gary Paulsen, *The River* (New York: Delacorte, 1991), 21; hereafter cited in the text as *River*.

5. Hanna B. Zeiger, review of *The River*, *Horn Book*, July/August 1991, 459.

6. Review of *The River*, *Publishers Weekly*, 31 May 1991, 76.

7. Gary Paulsen, *Father Water, Mother Woods: Essays on Fishing and Hunting in the North Woods* (New York: Delacorte, 1994), ix; hereafter cited in the text as *Father*.

8. Gary Paulsen, *The Voyage of the Frog* (New York: Orchard Books, 1989), 114; hereafter cited in the text as *Voyage*.

9. Review of *The Voyage of the Frog*, *School Library Journal*, January 1989, 94.

10.　Review of *The Voyage of the Frog*, *Bulletin of the Center for Children's Books*, January 1989, 131.

11.　Gary Paulsen, *The Haymeadow* (New York: Delacorte, 1992); hereafter cited in the text as *Haymeadow*.

12.　Review of *The Haymeadow*, *Publishers Weekly*, 1 June 1992, 64.

13.　Gary Paulsen, *Tracker* (New York: Bradbury Press, 1984), 76; hereafter cited in the text.

14.　Gary Paulsen, *Real Animals: The Grass Eaters* (Milwaukee: Raintree Editions, 1976), v.

15.　Gary Paulsen and Art Browne Jr., *TV and Movie Animals* (New York: Messner, 1980).

4. Becoming Whole: Paulsen's Novels of Maturation and Growth

1.　Kenneth L. Donelson and Alleen Pace Nilsen, *Literature for Today's Young Adults*, 3rd ed. (Glenview, Ill.: Scott Foresman, 1989), 23.

2.　Robert Cormier, *The Chocolate War* (New York: Random House, 1974), 97.

3.　Edwin J. Kenney Jr., review of *The Island*, *New York Times Book Review*, 22 May 1988.

4.　Review of *The Island*, *Bulletin of the Center for Children's Books*, May 1988, 186.

5.　Gary Paulsen, *The Island* (New York: Orchard Books, 1988), 8; hereafter cited in the text as *Island*.

6.　Gary Paulsen, *Dogsong* (New York: Bradbury Press, 1985), 9; hereafter cited in the text.

7.　Ethel R. Twichell, review of *Dogsong*, *Horn Book*, July/August 1985, 457.

8.　Gary Paulsen, *Canyons* (New York: Delacorte, 1990), 9; hereafter cited in the text.

5. Uncle, Teacher, Soldier: Paulsen's Mentor Stories

1.　Carolyn Meyer, "Wiseguides: Creating Adult Characters for Young Adult Readers," *Ohio Journal of the English Language Arts*, fall 1992, 10.

2.　Gary Paulsen, *Winterkill* (Nashville, Tenn.: Thomas Nelson, 1976), 142; hereafter cited in the text.

3.　Gary Paulsen, *Popcorn Days and Buttermilk Nights* (New York: E. P. Dutton, 1983), 57; hereafter cited in the text as *Popcorn*.

4. Review of *The Cookcamp, Publishers Weekly*, 14 December 1990, 67.

5. Carolyn D. Jenks, review of *The Cookcamp, Horn Book*, March/April 1991, 202.

6. Susan M. Harding, review of *The Cookcamp, School Library Journal*, February 1991, 82.

7. Patty Campbell, review of *The Cookcamp, New York Times Book Review*, 5 May 1991.

8. Gary Paulsen, *The Cookcamp* (New York: Orchard Books, 1991), 115; hereafter cited in the text as *Cookcamp*.

9. Gary Paulsen, *Nightjohn* (New York: Delacorte, 1993), 13; hereafter cited in the text.

10. Frances Bradburn, review of *Nightjohn, Wilson Library Bulletin*, January 1993, 88.

11. Gary Paulsen, *The Monument* (New York: Delacorte, 1991), 104; hereafter cited in the text as *Monument*.

12. Gary Paulsen, *Dancing Carl* (New York: Bradbury Press, 1983), 54; hereafter cited in the text as *Dancing*.

13. Gary Paulsen, *The Night the White Deer Died* (Nashville, Tenn.: Thomas Nelson, 1978), 55; hereafter cited in the text as *Night*.

14. Gary Paulsen, *The Foxman* (Nashville, Tenn.: Thomas Nelson, 1978), 37; hereafter cited in the text as *Foxman*.

15. Review of *The Foxman, Bulletin of the Center for Children's Books*, June 1977, 66.

16. Gary Paulsen, *The Crossing* (New York: Orchard Books, 1987), 14; hereafter cited in the text as *Crossing*.

17. Gary Paulsen, *Mr. Tucket*, rev. ed. (New York: Delacorte, 1994), 165; hereafter cited in the text as *Tucket*.

18. Gary Paulsen, *The Car* (New York: Harcourt Brace Jovanovich, 1994), 5; hereafter cited in the text as *Car*.

19. Alice Evans Handy, "An Interview with Gary Paulsen," *The Book Report* (May/June 1991): 30.

6. *Laughing, Roaring, Singing: Paulsen's Other Voices*

1. Gary Paulsen, *The Boy Who Owned the School* (New York: Orchard Books, 1990), 2; hereafter cited in the text as *Boy*.

2. Review of *The Boy Who Owned the School, Publishers Weekly*, 9 February 1990, 63.

3. Elizabeth A. Belden and Judith M. Beckman, review of *The Boy Who Owned the School, English Journal*, February 1991, 84.

4. Elizabeth S. Watson, review of *The Boy Who Owned the School, Horn Book*, July 1990, 458.

5. Gary Paulsen, *Sentries* (New York: Bradbury Press, 1986), 29.

6. Ronald Barron, "Gary Paulsen: 'I Write Because It's All I Can Do,'" *ALAN Review*, spring 1993, 29.

7. Review of *Sentries*, *Bulletin of the Center for Children's Books*, June 1986, 215.

8. Private conversation with Jennifer Flannery, Pittsburgh, 20 November 1993.

9. Gary Paulsen, *Sisters/Hermanas* (New York: Harcourt Brace Jovanovich, 1993), 26; hereafter cited in the text as *Sisters*.

10. Gary Paulsen, *The Winter Room* (New York: Orchard Books, 1989), 7; hereafter cited in the text as *Winter*.

11. Ethel R. Twichell, review of *The Winter Room*, *Horn Book*, March/April 1990, 209.

12. Review of *The Winter Room*, *Bulletin of the Center for Children's Books*, January 1990, 118.

13. Gary Paulsen, *Clabbered Dirt, Sweet Grass* (New York: Harcourt Brace Jovanovich, 1992), 19; hereafter cited in the text as *Clabbered*.

7. The Other Writer: Paulsen's Books for Adults and Young Children

1. Gary Paulsen, *Farm: A History and Celebration of the American Farmer* (Englewood Cliffs, N.J.: Prentice Hall, 1977), xii.

2. Debra Schneider, review of *Clabbered Dirt, Sweet Grass*, Library Journal, August 1992, 137.

3. Review of *Clabbered Dirt, Sweet Grass, Publishers Weekly*, 29 June 1992, 48.

4. Gary Paulsen, interview by Noah Adams, *All Things Considered* (National Public Radio, 1 October 1992); hereafter cited in the text as "NPR."

5. Review of *Night Rituals, Kirkus Reviews*, 15 May 1989, 724.

6. Sybil Steinberg, review of *Kill Fee, Publishers Weekly*, 22 June 1990, 46.

7. John F. Caviston, review of *Martin Luther King: The Man Who Climbed the Mountain, School Library Journal*, November 1976, 61.

8. The Now and Future Gary Paulsen: Today's Writing and Tomorrow's Plans

1. Franz Serdahely, "Prolific Paulsen," *Writer's Digest*, January 1980, 21.

Appendix: Honors and Prizes Won by Gary Paulsen

The Boy Who Owned the School

Parents' Choice Award, 1991
ALA Best Books for Young Adults, 1991

Canyons

ALA Best Book for Young Adults, 1990
New York Public Library, Books for the Teen Age Reader, 1991
Children's Booksellers Choice (Association of Booksellers for Children), 1991

The Car

American Booksellers "Pick of the Lists," spring 1994

The Cookcamp

American Booksellers "Pick of the Lists," 1991
ALA Best Book for Young Adults, 1992
School Library Journal Best Book of the Year, 1992

The Crossing

ALA Best Book for Young Adults, 1989
New York Public Library, Books for the Teen Age Reader, 1989

Dancing Carl

ALA Best Book for Young Adults, 1984
NCTE Notable Book in the Language Arts, 1984

Dogsong

Parent's Choice Award, 1985
Newbery Honor Book, 1986
ALA Notable Children's Book, 1986
ALA Best Book for Young Adults, 1986
School Library Journal Best Book of the Year, 1986
Child Study Association, Children's Book of the Year, 1986
Tennessee Volunteer State Book Award, 1989

Dogteam

IRA Children's Book Council, "Children's Choice for 1994"

Father Water, Mother Woods

Publishers Weekly Best Book of 1994

Harris and Me

New York Public Library, Children's Books: 100 Titles for Reading and
    Sharing, 1993
ALA Best Book for Young Adults, 1994
ALA Recommended Book for Reluctant Readers, 1994
Booklist Books for Youth, "Top of the List," 1993

Hatchet

Newbery Honor Book, 1988
Minnesota Book Award for Older Children, 1988
ALA Notable Children's Book, 1988
Booklist Editor's Choice, 1988
Vermont Dorothy Canfield Fisher Children's Book Award, 1989
Wisconsin Golder Archer Awards, 1989
Iowa Children's Choice Award and Iowa Teen Award, 1990
Kansas William Allen White Children's Book Award, 1990
North Dakota Flicker Tale Children's Book Award, 1990
Oklahoma Sequoia Children's and Young Adult Book Awards, 1990
Virginia Young Readers Program, 1990
Georgia Young Readers Program, 1990
Young Indiana Hoosier Book Awards, 1991
Minnesota Maud Hart Lovelace Book Award, 1991
Ohio Buckeye Children's Book Award, 1991
U.S. News and World Report Backlist Bestseller, 1992
NCTE Notable Book in Language Arts, 1989

The Haymeadow

ALA Best Book for Young Adults, 1993
Spur Award, Western Writers of America, 1993
New York Public Library, Books for the Teen Age Reader, 1993
Children's Booksellers Choice (Association of Booksellers for Children), 1993
Maine Student Book Award List, 1993–94
Young Indiana Hoosier Book Award List, 1994
Nebraska Young Golden Sower Award, 1994
Kansas William Allen White Award, 1994
Missouri Mark Twain Book Award, 1994
Texas Lonestar Reading Program, 1994
Illinois Rebecca Caudill Young Reader's Book Award, 1994
South Carolina Junior Book Award, 1994

The Island

ALA Best Book for Young Adults, 1989
NCTE Notable Trade Book in the Language Arts, 1989

The Monument

ALA Best Book for Young Adults, 1992
New York Public Library, Books for the Teen Age Reader, 1992
South Dakota Library Association, "Twenty Best Published Books in the Last Five Years," 1993

Nightjohn

Notable Children's Book in the Field of Social Studies, 1994
ALA Best Book for Young Adults, 1994
ALA Notable Children's Book, 1994
New York Public Library, Books for the Teen Age Reader, 1994
IRA Children's Book Council, "Children's Choice for 1994"

The River

Children's Booksellers Choice (Association of Booksellers for Children), 1992
New York Public Library, Books for the Teen Age Reader, 1992
Nebraska Golden Sower Award Program, 1993

Sentries

Notable Children's Trade Book in Social Studies, 1986

Sisters/Hermanas

American Booksellers "Pick of the Lists," 1993

Tracker

ALA Best Book for Young Adults, 1984
Society of Midland Authors Book Award, 1985

The Voyage of the Frog

School Library Journal Best Book of the Year, 1990
ALA Best Book for Young Adults, 1990
ALA Notable Children's Book, 1990
ALA Recommended Books for the Reluctant Young Reader, 1990
Parenting Magazine Reading-Magic Award/Top Ten Book, 1990
IRA Teachers' Choice, 1990
Learning Magazine Best Book of the Year, 1990

The Winter Room

Newbery Honor Book, 1990
Judy Lopez Memorial Award, 1990
Parents' Magazine Best Book of the Year, 1990
ALA Best Book for Young Adults, 1990
ALA Notable Children's Book, 1990
American Bookseller Pick of the Lists, 1989
NCTE Notable Trade Books in the Language Arts, 1990
IRA Children's Book Council, Favorite Paperback for 1994

Woodsong

American Bookseller Pick of the Lists, 1990
School Library Journal Best Book of the Year, 1990
Booklist Editor's Choice, 1991
ALA Best Books for Young Adults, 1991
ALA Notable Children's Book, 1991
ALA Recommended Books for the Reluctant Young Reader, 1991
Minnesota Book Award for Older Children, 1991
Society of Midland Authors Book Award, 1991
Western Writers of America Spur Award, 1991
New York Public Library, Books for the Teen Age Reader, 1991
NCTE Notable Book in the Language Arts, 1991

Selected Bibliography

Primary Sources

Young Adult Novels

The Boy Who Owned the School. New York: Orchard Books, 1990.
Canyons. New York: Delacorte, 1990.
The Car. New York: Harcourt Brace Jovanovich, 1994.
A Christmas Sonata. New York: Delacorte, 1992.
The Cookcamp. New York: Orchard Books, 1991.
The Crossing. New York: Orchard Books, 1987.
Dancing Carl. New York: Bradbury Press, 1983.
Dogsong. New York: Bradbury Press, 1985.
The Foxman. Nashville, Tenn.: Thomas Nelson, 1978.
Harris and Me. New York: Harcourt Brace Jovanovich, 1993.
Hatchet. New York: Bradbury Press, 1987.
The Haymeadow. New York: Delacorte, 1992.
The Island. New York: Orchard Books, 1988.
The Monument. New York: Delacorte, 1991.
Mr. Tucket, rev. ed. New York: Delacorte, 1994.
Nightjohn. New York: Delacorte, 1993.
The Night the White Deer Died. Nashville, Tenn.: Thomas Nelson, 1978.
Popcorn Days and Buttermilk Nights. New York: E. P. Dutton, 1983.
The River. New York: Delacorte, 1991.
Sentries. New York: Bradbury Press, 1986.
Sisters/Hermanas. New York: Harcourt Brace Jovanovich, 1993.
Tiltawhirl John. Nashville, Tenn.: Thomas Nelson, 1977.
Tracker. New York: Bradbury Press, 1984.
The Voyage of the Frog. New York: Orchard Books, 1989.
Winterkill. Nashville, Tenn.: Thomas Nelson, 1976.
The Winter Room. New York: Orchard Books, 1989.

Young Adult Nonfiction

Father Water, Mother Woods. New York: Delacorte, 1994.
Martin Luther King: The Man Who Climbed the Mountain. Milwaukee: Raintree Editions, 1976. (co-author with Dan Theis)
Real Animals: The Grass Eaters. Milwaukee: Raintree Editions, 1976.
Real Animals: The Small Ones. Milwaukee: Raintree Editions, 1976.
TV and Movie Animals. New York: Messner, 1980. (co-author with Art Browne Jr.)
Woodsong. New York: Bradbury/Macmillan, 1990.

Adult Fiction and Nonfiction

Clabbered Dirt, Sweet Grass. New York: Harcourt Brace Jovanovich, 1992.
Eastern Sun, Winter Moon. New York: Harcourt Brace Jovanovich, 1993.
Farm: A History and Celebration of the American Farmer. Englewood Cliffs, N.J.: Prentice Hall, 1977.
The Madonna Stories. New York: Harcourt Brace Jovanovich, 1989.
Winterdance: The Fine Madness of Running the Iditarod. New York: Harcourt Brace Jovanovich, 1994.

Secondary Sources

Books

Chevalier, Tracy, ed. *Twentieth Century Children's Writers*, 3rd ed. Chicago: St. James Press, 1989.
Collier, Laurie, and Joyce Nakamura, eds. *Major Authors and Illustrators for Children and Young Adults*, vol. 5. Detroit: Gale Research, 1993.
Commire, Anne, ed. *Something About the Author*, vol. 54. Detroit: Gale Research, 1989.
Donelson, Kenneth L., and Alleen Pace Nilson. *Literature for Today's Young Adults*. 3rd ed. Glenview, Ill.: Scott Foresman, 1989.
Garrett, Agnes, and Helga P. McCue, eds. *Authors and Artists for Young Adults*, vol 2. Detroit: Gale Research, 1989.
Senick, Gerard J., ed. *Children's Literature Review*, vol. 19. Detroit: Gale Research, 1990.

Articles

Barron, Ronald. "Gary Paulsen: 'I Write Because It's All I Can Do.'" *ALAN Review*, spring 1993: 27–30.

Davis, Rich. "North to Alaska." *Evansville Courier*, 8 March 1992.

Handy, Alice Evans. "An Interview with Gary Paulsen." *Book Report*, May/June 1991: 28–31.

Miller, Kay. "Suddenly Fame and Fortune." *Minneapolis Star-Tribune Sunday Magazine*, 10 July 1988.

Nelms, Elizabeth D. and Ben F. Nelms. "Gary Paulsen: The Storyteller's Legacy." *English Journal*, January 1992: 85–88.

Raymond, Allen. "Gary Paulsen: Artist-With-Words." *Teaching PreK–8*, August/September 1992: 52–54.

Roback, Diane. "Paulsen Inks Long-Term Deal with HB." *Publishers Weekly*, 8 February 1993: 10.

Serdahely, Franz. "Prolific Paulsen." *Writer's Digest*, January 1980: 20–21.

Unger, Jeff. "The Sage of Survival," *Entertainment*, 19 July 1991: 68–70.

Book Reviews

The Boy Who Owned the School
Belden, Elizabeth D., and Judith M. Beckman. *English Journal*, February 1991: 84.

Roback, Diane. *Publishers Weekly*, 9 February 1990: 63.

Schubert, Leda. *School Library Journal*, April 1990: 145.

Watson, Elizabeth S. *Horn Book*, July 1990: 458.

Canyons
Murphy, Susan. *Journal of Reading*, September 1991: 67.

Nelms, Elizabeth D., and Ben F. Nelms. *English Journal*, January 1992: 86–87.

Roback, Diane. *Publishers Weekly*, 13 July 1990: 56.

The Car
McBroom, Gerry. *ALAN Review*, fall 1994: 36.

Clabbered Dirt, Sweet Grass
Publishers Weekly, 29 June 1992: 48.

Schneider, Debra. *Library Journal*, August 1992: 137.

The Cookcamp
Bushman, John. *English Journal*, April 1992: 86.

Campbell, Patty. *New York Times Book Review*, 5 May 1991.

Harding, Susan. *School Library Journal*, February 1991: 82.

Jenks, Carolyn K. *Horn Book*, March/April 1991: 202.

Roback, Diane. *Publishers Weekly*, 14 December 1990: 67.

The Crossing
Bulletin of the Center for Children's Books, June 1988: 15–16.

Johnsen, Shirley. *English Journal*. January 1992: 86–87.

Twichell, Ethel R. *Horn Book*, November/December 1987: 744–45.

Dancing Carl
Bulletin of the Center for Children's Books, November 1983: 216.
Hand, Dorcas. *Horn Book*, August 1983: 446–47.
Kromann-Kelly, Inga. *Language Arts*, January 1984: 68.

Dogsong
Bulletin of the Center for Children's Books, April 1985: 174.
Twichell, Ethel R. *Horn Book*, July/August 1985: 456–57.

Eastern Sun, Winter Moon
Publishers Weekly, 25 January 1993: 73.
Zindel, Tim. *Library Journal*, 15 February 1993: 174.

Farm: A History and Celebration of the American Farmer
Booklist, 15 October 1977: 343.
Hodges, Louise. *Library Journal*, 1 October 1977: 2073.
Publishers Weekly, 15 August 1977: 62.

The Foxman
Booklist, 15 June 1977: 1576–77.
Bulletin of the Center for Children's Books, June 1977: 66.
Nelms, Elizabeth D., and Ben F. Nelms. *English Journal*, January 1992: 88.

Harris and Me
Duke, Charles R. *ALAN Review*, spring 1994: 40.

Hatchet
Abrahamson, Richard. *Journal of Reading*, March 1988: 579–80.
Bulletin of the Center for Children's Books, December 1987: 73.
Campbell, Patty. *Wilson Library Bulletin*, January 1988: 76.
English Journal, October 1988: 79.
Nelms, Elizabeth D., and Ben F. Nelms. *English Journal*, January 1992: 86.
Twichell, Ethel R. *Horn Book*, March/April 1988: 210–11.
Tucker, Nicholas. *Times Educational Supplement*, 17 November 1989.

The Haymeadow
Publishers Weekly, 1 June 1992: 63–64.
Zeiger, Hanna B. *Horn Book*, July 1992: 456.

The Island
Bigelow, Therese. *School Library Journal*, May 1988: 111–12.
Bulletin of the Center for Children's Books, May 1988: 186.
Kenney, Edwin J., Jr. *New York Times Book Review*, 22 May 1988.
Publishers Weekly, 11 March 1988, 105.
Twichell, Ethel R. *Horn Book*, May/June 1988: 361.

Kill Fee
Steinberg, Sybil. *Publishers Weekly*, 22 June 1990: 46.

Martin Luther King: The Man Who Climbed the Mountain
Booklist, 1 February 1977: 837.
Caviston, John F. *School Library Journal*, November 1976: 61.

The Monument
Nelms, Elizabeth D., and Ben F. Nelms. *English Journal*, January 1992: 88.

Mr. Tucket
Stanton, Susan. *Library Journal*, 15 December 1969: 4608.

Nightjohn
Bradburn, Frances. *Wilson Library Bulletin*, January 1993: 87–88.

Night Rituals
Kirkus Reviews, 15 May 1989: 724.

The Night the White Deer Died
Murphy, Susan. *Journal of Reading*, September 1991: 66–67.
Publishers Weekly, 11 December 1978: 69–70.

Popcorn Days and Buttermilk Nights
Bulletin of the Center for Children's Books, June 1984: 75.
Publishers Weekly, 27 October 1989: 72.

Real Animals: The Grass Eaters; Real Animals: The Small Ones
Hearne, Betsy. *Booklist*, 1 October 1976: 255.

The River
Bulletin of the Center for Children's Books, June 1991: 247.
Fader, Ellen. *School Library Journal*, May 1991: 112–13.
Meeker, Amy. *Publishers Weekly*, 26 July 1991: 12.
Publishers Weekly, 31 May 1991: 76.
Zeiger, Hanna B. *Horn Book*, July/August 1991: 459.

Sentries
Bulletin of the Center for Children's Books, June 1986: 215.
Lilja, Linnea, Mark Vogel, and Don Zancanella, *English Journal*, March 1987: 105.
Orgel, Doris. *New York Times Book Review*, 29 June 1986.
Publishers Weekly, 9 October 1987: 91.

Sisters/Hermanas
Hipple, Ted. *ALAN Review*, fall 1994: 38.

Tracker
Bulletin of the Center for Children's Books, June 1984: 172.
Horn Book, June 1984: 340–41.

The Voyage of the Frog
Bulletin of the Center for Children's Books, January 1989: 131.
Burns, Connie Tyrrell. *School Library Journal*, January 1989: 94.
Publishers Weekly, 23 December 1988: 83.
Reading Teacher, November 1990: 236.
Twichell, Ethel R. *Horn Book*, March/April 1989: 219.

Winterkill
Booklist, 15 April 1977: 1268.

The Winter Room
Bradburn, Frances. *Wilson Library Bulletin*, November 1989: 94.
Bulletin of the Center for Children's Books, January 1990: 118.
Mambi, Nancy. *Five Owls*, January/February 1990: 42.
Nelms, Elizabeth D., and Ben F. Nelms. *English Journal*, January 1992: 88.
Rees, David. *Times Literary Supplement*, 15 July 1977.
Twichell, Ethel R. *Horn Book*, March/April 1990: 209.
Whalin, Kathleen. *Language Arts*, September 1990: 427–28.

Woodsong
Booklist, 15 March 1991: 1472.
Bulletin of the Center for Children's Books, October 1990: 41.
Fraser, Stephen. *Five Owls*, November/December 1990: 35.
Language Arts, September 1991: 398.
McNulty, Faith. *New Yorker*, 26 November 1990: 144.
Nilsen, Alleen Pace, and Ken Donelson, *English Journal*, December 1991: 84.
Parents Magazine, December 1990: 202, 206.
Publishers Weekly, 27 July 1990: 234–35.
Vasilakis, Nancy. *Horn Book*, November/December 1990: 763.

Index

The Author

A former elementary and secondary school teacher, Gary Salvner is currently Professor of English Education at Youngstown State University, where he teaches courses in children's and adolescent literature and in the teaching of English. He was a member of the Board of Directors of the Assembly on Literature for Adolescents of the National Council of Teachers of English (ALAN) and currently co-edits the Book Review section of the *ALAN Review*. Salvner is the former editor of the *Ohio Journal of the English Language Arts* and co-editor of the book *Reading Their World: The Young Adult Novel in the Classroom*. Twice a recipient of his university's Distinguished Professor Award, he also was honored in 1993 as Ohio College English Teacher of the Year.

The Editor

Patricia J. Campbell is an author and critic specializing in books for young adults. She has taught adolescent literature at UCLA and was formerly the assistant coordinator of young adult services for the Los Angeles Public Library. Her literary criticism has been published in the *New York Times Book Review* and many other journals. From 1978 to 1988 her column "The YA Perplex," a monthly review of young adult books, appeared in the *Wilson Library Bulletin*. She now writes a review column on the independent press for that magazine, and a column on controversial issues in adolescent literature for *Horn Book*. Campbell is the author of five books, among them *Presenting Robert Cormier*, the first volume in the Twayne Young Adult Authors Series. In 1989 she was the recipient of the American Library Association Grolier Award for distinguished achievement with young people and books. A native of Los Angeles, Campbell now lives on an avocado ranch near San Diego, where she and her husband, David Shore, write and publish books on overseas motorhome travel.